WORKING WITH
PEOPLE
CALLED
PATIENTS

Some Remedies for "Madness" Prescribed in the Middle Ages

"... that noble and famous confection Alkermes, made by the Arabians, containing the grains of the scarlet oak. It is good against melancholy deseases, vaine imaginations, sighings, griefe and sorrow without manifest cause, for that it purgeth away melancholy humors."

"Poultices applied to the head, of mustard and figs, are recommended for epilepsy and lethargy."

"... double yellow and white batchelor's buttons, hung 'in a linnen cloath about the necke of him that is lunaticke, in the waine of the moone, when the signe shall be in the first degree of Taurus or Scorpio.'"

"... emetics, purges, opening the veins under the tongue, blisters, and shaving the head, followed by a cataplasm upon it, the backbone anointed with a very choice balsam of earthworms or bats."

One prescription for melancholia contains no less than 27 ingredients, "... to be added that sine qua non, the ever precious hellebore."

Other remedies prescribed in some cases were the "bezoartick pastills," composed of an immense number of ingredients, including the skull of a stag and of a healthy man who had been executed. The commentary triumphantly made by this lover of polypharmacy in the middle ages when this medicine was administered, runs thus: "These things being exactly performed, this noble gentleman was cured."°

°From *Chapters in the History of the Insane in the British Isles* by Daniel Hack Tuke, M.D., F.R.C.P. (Kegan Paul, Trench & Co., London, 1882).

WORKING WITH

People
Called
Patients

---

by

MILTON M. BERGER, M.D.

Director of Education and Training,
South Beach Psychiatric Center, Staten Island, New York
Clinical Associate Professor of Psychiatry,
Downstate Medical Center, S.U.N.Y., Brooklyn, New York

BRUNNER/MAZEL, *Publishers* • **NEW YORK**

To My Grandchildren
Elise, Jim, Daniel, Jennifer
and Matthew-John

FOURTH PRINTING

Library of Congress Cataloging in Publication Data

Berger, Milton Miles.
  Working with people called patients.

  Bibliography: p. 145
  Includes index.
  1. Psychiatry.   2. Allied mental health personnel.
I. Title.
RC454.B4545   616.8′9   76-46483
ISBN 0-87630-126-X

Published by
BRUNNER/MAZEL, INC.
19 Union Square, New York, N.Y. 10003

If I am not for myself, who is for me?
And being only for my own self, what am I?
And if not now, when?

Rabbi Hillel: The Talmud
Ethics of the Fathers

Foreword

In response to the increasing demand for psychotherapy, professionals have in recent years recruited and trained an army of para- and sub-professionals, including medical students, who participate in various therapeutic activities as part of their training. These activities include supportive therapy, counselling, patient advocacy and other therapeutic roles in clinics, hospitals, community mental health centers and other agencies.

Their greater closeness to patients in background and life-style often enables para- and sub-professionals to understand patients more intuitively, to represent more useful models for them to emulate, and to offer more acceptable advice and guidance. As a result, their effectiveness has been well established.

At the same time, the beginning therapist may easily be bewildered by conflicting doctrines and therapeutic methods, especially when faced with problems or clinical conditions for which the particular theory and method of his training program has ill prepared him. An insight-oriented approach may be poorly suited to a drug addict; a behavioral one, to an anxious college student.

Under these circumstances, a wise and experienced guide at one's side, who offers sound, practical, detailed advice on how to help patients who come or are brought to psychotherapy, can be invaluable. Dr. Berger is such a guide. In this manual he has distilled a professional lifetime of experience with individual and group therapies offered to persons in a wide variety of treatment settings, presenting just about every condition that a therapist is apt to encounter. The coverage is broadly inclusive, including characteristics of healthy as well as pathological functioning, community psychiatry and mental health careers. While the manual is intended primarily for the beginner, experienced therapists will find many astute clinical insights and ingenious therapeutic interventions.

Based on many years' experience teaching students with a wide range of educational backgrounds and clinical sophistication, the exposition is lucid, free of jargon and refreshingly informal. The reader often has the sense of being in face-to-face communication with the author. The mode of presentation is varied to fit the topic, and the material is presented in bite-size portions to facilitate assimilation.

In order to keep his intellectual bearings in the chaotic sea of psychotherapy, the practitioner needs a theoretical and descriptive framework. Consistent with his approach to patients as people, Dr. Berger's is primarily in terms of the many ways in which troubled persons can express the same underlying attitudes. At the same time, he provides enough formal classification and description for clinical purposes. In the present state of the art, no one can write a book in which every statement commands universal agreement of experts, but Dr. Berger has succeeded to a remarkable degree in hewing to a middle course which will secure the agreement of most experienced therapists.

Consistent with the view that successful psychotherapy requires that patients be approached not as specimens of psycho-pathology but as suffering persons wrestling with problems of living or with distressing and incapacitating symptoms, the manual stresses throughout working with healthy aspects of persons and protecting their self-esteem. Every page conveys an attitude of understanding, compassion and respect, which is the hallmark of the successful psychotherapist.

JEROME D. FRANK, M.D.
Professor Emeritus of Psychiatry
The Henry Phipps Psychiatric Clinic
The Johns Hopkins University
School of Medicine

Contents

Preface

This handbook is based on my 35 years as a psychiatrist in all types of settings, experiencing all types of patients. I have been involved in educational, training and treatment programs for professionals and paraprofessionals, for graduate students and laymen, for patients and their families, and for educators, lawyers, clergymen, and others who work with persons having emotional problems.

This handbook is to be your guide—to convey basic information to help in your understanding and approach to people with emotional and/or mental problems whether these persons are patients, clients, or those not yet "labeled" as patients or clients. It is written to help those planning on careers as mental health workers, whether their work be as aides or mental health therapists, in inpatient or outpatient settings, with the old or young. It can be read profitably by anyone inexperienced in dealing with those suffering emotional-mental disorders.

It finally dawned on many of us professionals that much of what we've learned as psychiatrists, psychologists and social workers could be learned and practiced in whole or in part by all others working in mental health settings. It was necessary to take sometimes esoteric concepts and abstract or condense them into different language forms, such as the language used with students in my courses on "Working With People Called Patients." We've learned to use diagrams, pictures and role-playing more often to teach concepts of what is pro-therapeutic and what is anti-therapeutic in a way which allows for experiential as well as intellectual learning.

Many of us realized in the last 15 years that the psychotherapeutic methods of exploration and confrontation were too good to be reserved for patients alone, so we expanded these techniques to groups of young and older persons interested in awareness, encounter, experimentation, change, maturation, and development of potential.

I have tried to cover in as simple a fashion as possible many complicated theoretical and practical formulations which I have learned to be of value during my lifetime. I know that mental health workers can help people because I was helped. The personal communications which I received from my teacher, Karen Horney, as well as from my therapist had profound impact when they hit me in my "guts" and radiated to the "all and everything" of me.

XI

The basic interpersonal atmosphere which needs to be developed between the person called "patient" and the person called "helper" is one of "I'm OK—You're OK—I'm With You." The basic process has two major components:

1. systems of undermining psychopathology;
2. systems of offering a constructive emotional and educational experience in a trusting relationship.

The book is intended for professionals, paraprofessionals and students in the fields of psychiatry, general medicine, psychology, social work, nursing or rehabilitation. In addition, it is hoped that it will be helpful to patients and to families of people called patients, as well as to educators, attorneys, clergy and all others who work with or have a relationship with persons having emotional, mental or behavioral problems. And, finally, it can be a source book for those who write on *"the human condition."*

Acknowledgments

I dedicate this book to all those who came before me to reach their hands and hearts toward the emotionally, mentally and physically "lame, halt and blind."

I have been influenced by and dedicate this book to the legendary Aesculapius who long before the Christian era provided a sanctuary for rest and warm baths "for the disturbed"; to Pinel who unlocked the chains of the brutalized patients at Salpêtrière in Paris in 1793; to Liébault and Bernheim at their clinic in Nancy, France, who demonstrated the power of positive thinking, hope and suggestion in the 1880's; to Freud, Jung, Adler, Reich, Ferenczi, Sullivan and Horney, who helped us understand in depth what many wise men had known intuitively for thousands of years—that what goes on in our minds during childhood and what goes into our minds and bodies from our families, schools, churches, and society while we are children influence and mold our character structure and personality till the end of our days; to Clifford W. Beers (author in 1908 of *A Mind That Found Itself*), who used his own experience as a hospitalized patient after the turn of this century as a stepping-stone (with the support and help of Dr. Adolf Meyer, dean of American psychiatry) to create The National Committee for Mental Hygiene;° to Albert Deutsch,°° the writer of *Bedlam* in the 1950's, who, over and over again, exposed the shameful and dehumanizing conditions in our large state mental hospitals; to all those who worked on the Joint Commission for the Study of Mental Illness and then prepared the ten monographs on "Action for Mental Health"°°° which sparked today's Community Psychiatry Treatment and Prevention Programs.

° In 1908 he founded The Connecticut Society for Mental Health and by 1909 gained enough support for his objectives to launch the National Committee for Mental Hygiene whose chief purposes were ". . . to work for the conservation of mental health; to help prevent nervous and mental disorders and mental defects; to help raise the standards of care for those suffering from any of these disorders or defects; to secure and disseminate reliable information on these subjects; to cooperate with federal, state and local agencies or officials and with public and private agencies whose work is in any way related to that of a society for mental hygiene." See pp. 303-394, section on "The Mental Hygiene Movement (1908-1933) And Its Founder" by C. E. A. Winslow in *A Mind That Found Itself* by Clifford W. Beers, Revised Edition 1971, Doubleday & Company, New York.

°° *The Mentally Ill In America*, 2nd Ed., Columbia University Press, New York, 1949.

°°° *Action for Mental Health*, Basic Books, New York, 1961.

I dedicate this book to all my teachers and students in many settings who have forced me to clarify my feelings and thoughts. I thank Dr. Walter L. Moore of St. Louis, who inspired my formal interest in psychiatry and gave me a major "group" experience when he assigned me to 900 patients in the St. Louis City Sanitarium (now St. Louis State Hospital) in 1942, and also Dr. Harold Kelman of New York City who fostered in me an appreciation for acceptance of process and systems and self which goes beyond such everyday judgmental values as "good-bad" or "right-wrong" while expanding the search for the "what-is-ness" of everyday life in helping me to learn to enjoy what there is to enjoy.

I dedicate this book to Dr. Alan Miller, former Commissioner of the New York State Department of Mental Hygiene, and Dr. Alvin M. Mesnikoff, former Director of South Beach Psychiatric Center, for providing me with the opportunity to join with them in fulfilling their dream and the dream of so many others who believed there could be such a high quality, enlightened provider of comprehensive human services as the South Beach Psychiatric Center on Staten Island, New York.

And finally I dedicate this book to all my patients, past and present, who have helped me to learn more about myself as well as them—sometimes by stimulation and sometimes by provocation.

My heartfelt thanks go to all those who helped me in the writing of this volume: my wife Lynne Flexner Berger who supported my basic beliefs and philosophies while helping as my most caring critic; Pat Corbitt, Fran Arje and Joanna Steichen who made sensitive suggestions to clarify content; Jay Amberson, medical student at Johns Hopkins, for reading the manuscript and making valuable suggestions and criticisms; Donald Cisyk and Millie Montagna who contributed the resources of the South Beach Psychiatric Center Library; Alice Erdmann, Grace Castelli and Ann Mericko who shepherded the manuscript through many typings; and my editor Susan Barrows who worked closely with me in creating the form for presentation of my content and made many other invaluable suggestions to add to the comprehensiveness of this book.

MILTON M. BERGER, M.D.

WORKING WITH
PEOPLE
CALLED
PATIENTS

1
The "Evil Eye" and Other "Truths"

In the early days of recorded history and even up to recent times, hysterical reactions and many varieties of psychotic behaviors were often thought to be due to diabolical or demonic possession. It was the concept of being possessed by evil spirits which led the residents of Salem, Massachusetts, in the 18th century to condemn many persons as "witches" because they were accused of having the "evil eye." They were then flogged and burned to death. And many religious Jews believed that those who did not conform to their families' beliefs and behaved in other strange ways were possessed by the "Dybbuk."

In more recent times, general interest in the strange and often bizarre functioning of the mentally disturbed led to the amazing popularity of "The Exorcist," a film which showed the efforts of Catholic clergymen to get rid of the "devil" which had taken up residence in a young girl and made her act in strange and maniacal ways.

The idea that insane people were inhabited by demons, witches and other evil spirits led primitive medicine men or "shamans" to cut holes in the skulls of such unfortunate afflicted tribesmen while the tribal "team" sang, danced, shouted, struck gongs and bells, and made multiple efforts, usually at the time of the full moon, to frighten, shock, or otherwise drive the evil spirits out of the body of the inhabited person through the holes they had trephined.

If we believe that the methods of the shamans were simplistic, we must be open to the awareness that there was a considerable body of scientific and medico-surgical experience behind the decision to perform prefrontal lobotomies on selected patients in the 1940's and early 1950's of this century right here in the United States. These operations were decided upon solely as a method of handling unmanageable patients who could not be controlled in any other fashion except by being constantly kept in leather or iron shackles, straitjackets or wet sheet packs. Such patients often had been homicidal as well as suicidal, and had not responded favorably to hundreds of insulin-coma and/or electroconvulsive "shock" treatments which were somewhat effective in quieting most unmanageable, disturbed, and agitated patients in hospitals at that time.

After experiments on monkeys and gorillas showed that prefrontal lobotomies

tion produced irreversible changes and that some of those operated on lost their capacity for "joie de vivre" or their "élan vital," sitting around afterwards like "vegetables." The operation consisted of cutting fibers in the prefrontal lobes of the brain so that patients, even when they were aware of disturbing inner or outer stimuli, no longer reacted with inappropriate or excessively destructive rage. It offered a way to manage raging and unmanageable persons without keeping them in isolation or continuously drugged into a "near-zombie" state.

Since the development of predictable, relatively safe chemicals and psychotropic drugs (those which act on the central nervous system) in the last quarter-century, there has been a tremendous surge in the capacity of all physicians (not only psychiatrists) to help people cope with excessive emotional or physical reactions to acute or chronic stressful situations or inner conflicts. Just as we've given up the leather and iron restraints formerly used to tie or chain patients, we have also been able to give up most of our use of lobotomies, and much of our use of electro-convulsive and insulin-coma therapy. However, electro-convulsive and insulin-coma therapy still have lifesaving value for certain suicidal and schizophrenic patients who have not been helped by psychotropic drugs or by individual, group, or family therapy, alone or in combination.

When appropriately prescribed, the newly developed medications can reduce anxiety, agitation, depression, insomnia, withdrawal, hallucinations, delusions, and suicidal and homicidal impulses. They can promote an inner calm, sleep, better mood, and a desire to communicate, to cooperate, and to get out of bed to face the reality of daily living. However, we must be alert to the practice in some institutions of "drugging" patients with the new medi-

could reduce behavioral raging in animals stimulated to maximum anger, the operation was performed on thousands of patients in public and private hospitals. The results were that one-third of those persons operated on became well enough to be discharged from the hospital to go back to live with their families; another third improved sufficiently to become manageable, though still remaining in the hospital; the remaining third showed no improvement. The major criticisms were that the opera-

cines (a "psychotropic lobotomy") to keep them quiet and manageable rather than providing other more costly and time-consuming treatment services such as psychotherapy. (See page 60 on the new medicines.)

We've come a long way in our understanding of what causes disturbed thinking, feeling, perception, and behaviors. And we've come a long way with techniques for crisis intervention and with the treatment approaches we now have available in the community as well as in hospitals.

It is absolutely necessary that we share and apply this knowledge which has medical, psychological and social aspects and applications.

There is hope for the mentally disabled if we reach toward them consistently and in a unified fashion with knowledge, with empathy, with sureness, with mutuality, and with a high level of interest and positive regard.

2 Who Could Become a Mental Patient?

Kings and Congressmen

Cabinet Ministers and Cab Drivers

Princes and Paupers

Princesses and Prostitutes

Housewives and Hardhats

Soldiers and Civilians

Students and Teachers

Young and Old

Marrieds and Singles

Models and Ugly Ducklings

Whites, Blacks, and All Others

The Genius and the Average Person and the Mentally Retarded

The Overprotected and the Underprivileged

The College Graduate and the High School Drop-out

The Rich and the Poor

Grandparents—Parents—Children

Native-born and Immigrants

Suburbanites and City Dwellers

Movie Stars and Office Workers

The causes of mental illness are multiple. These factors mutually influence each other in all individuals, families, and cultures:

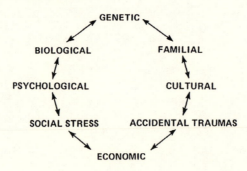

3

Myths About the Mentally Ill

For all too many years now, the basic beliefs of many people concerning patients in mental hospitals have been that:

1. "Mental patients are irresponsible."

2. "Mental patients are more liable than others to harm themselves."

3. "Mental patients are *all* prone to act violently."

4. "Most mental patients suffer from a chronic illness and are unlikely to improve."

5. "Patients don't know what is good for them and, therefore, they are to be treated as objects or children rather than as persons."

6. "Most mental patients are not in touch with reality so there's no use talking to them about everyday things. Just order them to do things. They are not as sensitive about most things as the rest of us are."

All these assumptions have caused untold misery and cruelty for millions of people. *For the most part they are false!* Let's examine some truths!

1. Most people become mental patients because they are unable to cope with or adapt to the stresses and problems of everyday life—at home, at school, at work, or socially!

2. While a small percentage of patients have made harmful moves toward themselves or others, the majority are basically shy and self-effacing, and only acted out violently when *provoked excessively or taunted cruelly or repeatedly demeaned and put down* to a terribly humiliating degree.

3. While mental patients are often irresponsible, screaming and sometimes violently out of control when first brought to a crisis center or to an emergency room, they can, with appropriate intervention, very quickly reintegrate their control systems, and stop efforts to harm themselves or others.

4. Most patients who have not be-

come permanently hopeless, helpless, and chronically regressed or withdrawn as a consequence of long-term hospitalization and inhuman custodial incarceration are able to be rehabilitated through active psychotherapy, psychopharmacological medications, and resocializing and rehabilitative activity programs. They can then be discharged to outpatient day centers or sheltered workshops, admitted to residential homes or halfway house programs, or returned to their family. The average hospitalization time of new patients in New York State Psychiatric Centers such as South Beach runs from 7 to 50 days because of such continuity of care. It may average 40 to 75 days in other hospitals with different treatment philosophy and post-hospitalization arrangements.

5. When patients are treated as objects, they cannot build up or renew a feeling of self-esteem or significance as a person or develop self-respect. When patients are treated as people, i.e., with interest—with understanding—with education—with communication—and with compassion and regard for their personhood, they react as persons and develop or rebuild self-esteem, self-confidence, and a capacity for trusting and being responsible for themselves and for others, whether those others are other patients, members of staff, or family.

6. Patients are like you and me. More often than given credit for, they have the sense and awareness to have rational personal tastes, wants, and wishes, to show sensitivity on all levels, and to respond to "t.l.c." (tender loving care) and personalized interest as do the rest of us. Yes! Patients are like you and me. Patients are People!

Let us remember John Donne's words:

"No man is an Iland, intire of itselfe . . ."

and also that:

"There but for the grace of God go I."

4 Some Basic Facts About Mental Illness

- At any one moment, there are more people in hospitals for mental illness than people with all other diseases combined —including heart disease, cancer, tuberculosis or alcoholism.

- At least one person in every ten (and probably more) has enough mild to severe emotional or mental disability to require treatment. And probably one out of every two or three people could profit from individual or group counseling or treatment. And one family in every four has or will have an emotionally or mentally ill member who is hospitalized for a short or long period.

- Most of the diseases and symptoms of the body which plague people, such as high blood pressure, asthma, colitis, ulcers, constipation, headaches, sexual dysfunctions, and backaches have a large emotional component as their cause.

- All people have symptoms and problems reflecting that all is not *always* 100% perfect with the functioning of our minds, our bodies or our spirits—but that is not necessarily a sign of a diagnosable sickness. Such aches, pains, and problems are evidence of the "human condition."

They are evidence that no one's life is *always* easy, happy, or perfect.

- Most people with mental or emotional illness can be helped, through the efforts of professionals and paraprofessionals, to be educated toward change and to so alter their lives that they no longer require the perpetuation of their conscious and unconscious crippling and self-defeating neurotic or psychotic systems. Neurotic patterns adopted and developed and incorporated in childhood in order to adapt to troubling situations at that time can be identified and given up at a later time.

- All mental illness is not inherited. While there are substantial data to indicate a partially genetic factor as *one of the bases* for emotional and mental illness in some people, there is no clear-cut evidence that it is *the* causative factor in all people who suffer from an episode of mental illness. At this time there is a basis for believing in partial genetic causation for some forms of schizophrenia and manic-depressive illness. Such psychoses can also occur in persons exposed to toxic substances and extremely traumatic stressful situations such as occur

9

in wartime or when there is an unexpected loss of one or more loved family members. In working with people called patients, we can generally assume that the psychiatric disability is not caused by genetic factors and that the illness is usually curable.

Since most mental illness is not due to inherited factors, the children of people called patients do not have to fear that they have inherited mental illness. Environmental and familial factors are more important.

5

Comparing Non-patients and Patients

It is important to gain the clearest conception of the similarities and the differences between ourselves and those people we call patients.

Patients often show *inappropriate behaviors*—behaviors that are irrational, that *just don't make sense* to ordinary people. They manifest behavior that is not in context—that is out of place—that just doesn't seem right in this situation with these people. It's due to the fact that patients have distortions in their perceptions, their feelings, and their thoughts in a situation they are in and these repeated distortions can lead to disturbed behavior, which may drive other people away from them.

By *inappropriateness* we mean that there is an overreaction, underreaction, or unusual reaction in everyday life situations in or outside the hospital. This may show itself in remarks, attitudes, feelings, or behaviors. Patients show varying degrees of impairment in their ability to assess reality and to act according to what is realistic. Such impairment may be due to such common mental mechanisms as denial, distortion, projection (see pages 129 to 131 for complete list and definitions). These and other mechanisms may lead to distrustful, suspicious thinking to the point where the individual is considered to

suffer from segmental (partial) or massive areas of paranoid (persecutory) thinking which may lead to potential danger to oneself, to others, or to property. Various degrees and kinds of thought disorders, delusions, and auditory or visual hallucinations may also be present in such patients. Emotionally, patients may show an excess of flatness, depression, lability, euphoria, or hypomania.

Non-patients may also go through any of the above mentioned experiences at times, but they usually consider such momentary thoughts or feelings as "crazy" or "funny" or "odd." *The crazy thoughts and feelings do not become their own reality.* They do not become obsessed with or feel taken over by such thoughts, nor do they repeatedly feel driven to react unrealistically in everyday life because of such thoughts. *They maintain their contact with reality.*

A popular joke states "the neurotic builds castles in the air, the psychotic lives in them and the psychiatrist collects the rent." It is clear in this joke that the psychotic has lost his contact with reality to such a degree that he behaves according to the dictates of his thoughts or fantasies which now direct him. A neurotic person or a non-patient usually knows the difference

11

between the facts of reality and fantasy although he is sometimes reckless enough or risk-taking enough to act on his fantasy. If successful he may be considered "creative," "adventurous" or "pioneering." If he fails he may be considered "foolish," "wild" or "a little crazy."

Some examples of inappropriate behavior are:

1. A person talking out loud while walking along the street, seemingly unaware of his or her impact on others.

2. The person who is clothed with heavy overcoat, gloves, hat, scarves and earmuffs while walking in the park on a warm June day.

6 Patients Are Whole Persons — Not Objects

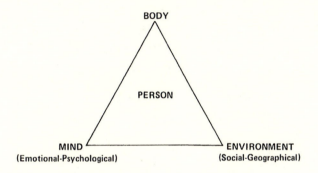

BODY

PERSON

MIND
(Emotional-Psychological)

ENVIRONMENT
(Social-Geographical)

The psychiatric patient is not someone to whom something is "done," as occurs in the usual medical situation. The psychiatric patient is encouraged to develop greater awareness of the functioning of his whole self. He learns that "all and everything" is important, e.g., that his sleeplessness and nocturnal anxiety, his cardiac palpitation, his gastrointestinal upset may be clearly related to the unexpressed anger and frustration he was feeling the evening before in a conversation with his wife, his teenage daughter, or his boss. He learns firsthand, rather than from a textbook, what is meant by psychosomatization (which is the expression through the body of emotional conflict or stress) and that he cannot act as if his daily thoughts, feelings, and life experiences in the world-at-large had nothing to do with his body function and symptom development.

In everyday life we hear people saying:

— "He was so worried his hair turned grey overnight."

— "His face was red with rage."

— "Her heart raced with anticipation and excitement."

— "He stood silent and stunned with fists clenched."

— "He felt so angry his stomach was tied up in a knot."

13

— "His anxiety was so great that his breathing was deep and rapid."

— "She paced back and forth with impatience."

— "He was so eager to prove his manliness that he had a premature ejaculation."

— "Her head pounded with rage that she couldn't express because of her fear of abandonment."

— "She was stooped over because of her depression."

— "He was so angry he broke out in a rash."

— "She was so anxious about passing the examination that she had butterflies in her stomach."

— "He had loose stools before giving the talk to his class."

7

What Is Mental Health?

In 1948, during its formative period, the World Federation for Mental Health gave us this definition of mental health:

> "1. Mental health is a condition which permits the optimal development, physical, intellectual and emotional, of the individual, so far as this is compatible with that of other individuals.
>
> 2. A good society is one that allows this development to its members while at the same time ensuring its own development and being tolerant toward other societies."

In 1957, The American Psychiatric Association published its first edition of "A Psychiatry Glossary," and under *"mental health,"* on page 43, it says *"See emotional health."* Under that heading on page 31, it says:

> *"emotional health:*
> A state of being which is relative rather than absolute, in which a person has effected a reasonably satisfactory integration of his instinctual drives. His integration is acceptable to himself and to his social milieu as reflected in the satisfactory nature of his interpersonal relationships, his level of satisfaction in living, his actual achievement, his flexibility, and the level of emotional maturity he has attained."

The third edition, published in 1969, has essentially the same definition but lists it under *"mental health"* on page 58. The fourth edition published in 1975 is almost the same, but ends with the statement: *". . . and the level of maturity he has attained,"* thus indicating that the maturity referred to is more comprehensive in what it embraces than the "emotional" maturity as specified in the first and third editions of this psychiatric glossary.°

Throughout the concepts of mental health and its opposite, mental illness, there runs the requirement that behavior is screened through the degree of its appro-

---

° The A.P.A. Psychiatric Glossary, 1975 Edition, also contains comprehensive tables of: Drugs used in psychiatry; Legal terms important in psychiatry; Neurological deficits; Research terms; Schools of Psychiatry; Psychological tests—including their names, types and what they assess in which ages of persons; Sleep Disorders.

priateness and acceptability in a specific society at a specific time in history to determine whether it is healthy or not. We see, then, that there is a broad sociological basis for both diagnosing and accepting and treating human behaviors. We see that the medical model is helpful in understanding and treating some mental and emotional disorders, but that the sociological approach is always important in our working with people called patients.

In Scotland there is the expression "He's no' wise" to describe those persons whose peculiar behavior is socially unacceptable—in that society! *We must keep in mind that in different societies there are different values and customs and concepts as to what constitutes mental illness.* This fact must be kept in front of us when we assess the individual patient, his family, his "symptoms," and the plan for his treatment.

Every society has popular or folk words to describe those of its members who are "not quite right in their head."

In English we have many such terms, perhaps because we have so many varieties of craziness in our complex society. We have "crazy"—"mad"—"batty"—"nuts"—"screwy"—"balmy"—"lunatic" and many more.

In other languages we have these:
Yiddish: *meshuga*
French: *fou* or *folle*
Italian: *pazzo, pazzamente, pazzesco, spustato*
Spanish: *loco*
German: *verrückt*
Russian: *bezumnyi, sumasshedshyi, pomeshanyi*
Polish: *zwarjowany*
Ukranian: *boshevilyi, dumyi, durak*

A Russian proverb is: "Everybody goes out of his mind in his own way."

In many parts of the world adherence is still given to the concept that a specific thought, feeling, or act is *always right* or *always wrong!* Such beliefs are still passed from one generation to another by many clergymen, "medicine men" and other "gurus" and by the masses who turn to them for the definition of "right" behavior or for the clarification and confirmation of the meaning of their existence. People who are obsessed with doing the "right" thing are plagued with indecision, guilt and self-hate.

In almost all societies *adaptive* behavior is behavior which for the most part conforms to the patterns of values accepted by the largest number of the most responsible persons in the society. And *maladaptive* or *deviant* behavior is that which does not fit in with social expectations. Thus, the maladaptive person arranges, through his own behavior, to be reproached, rejected, avoided, ignored, or, if his behavior bothers enough people, locked up involuntarily in a jail or in a mental hospital.

All too often, creative, inventive individuals who differ in their thinking and vary from the social majority may be ostracized and called "crazy" because their ideas are different. Frequently, these persons are ahead of their time and should, if possible, be differentiated from those who are truly "maladaptive." Individuals who are different are "variant" rather than "deviant."

In many towns and cities in the United States, it is the policeman who is called to deal not only with violent persons but also with deviant persons. This lack of differentiation between those individuals whose inappropriate appearance or behavior is due to emotional or mental illness and those individuals whose behavior is due to criminal intent continues to cause untold misery to many people who may be thrown into jail instead of being referred to a doctor or psychiatric facility.

However, recent United States Supreme Court decisions concerning the right to treatment for those who have previously been "warehoused" in mental institutions involuntarily for indeterminate years have brought about another revolution in terms of the rights of patients. The civil rights movement has been an important stimulus in the move for adequate care and treatment for those committed involuntarily and for those who have signed themselves into hospitals voluntarily. (See page 132 on *Patients' Bill of Rights* and page 134 on *Right to Treatment.*)

8 The Range Of Normality and Mental Health

People considered normal or healthy in one society or group might be considered abnormal, unhealthy or deviant in another society. There is no one definition of a "normal person" applicable to all people, at all times, in all situations.

It is a mistake to equate the "normal" person with the ideal or idealized one. People who function within the designation "healthy" are also imperfect, make mistakes, have "crazy thoughts" at times, have inner conflicts, and are not *absolutely* aware, honest, reliable, or responsible *all* the time.

Upon deep reflection I am compelled to state unequivocally that the idea of a *totally normal person* is not grounded in reality. From a realistic viewpoint, the concept of a healthy or normal person covers a wide area of human functioning and adaptation. The healthier a person, the greater is his adaptive capacity to integrate and react rationally or appropriately to unexpected, changing, or stressful events in his environment. Normality is to be strived for, although never absolutely achieved. We only know people who are *more-or-less* normal.

NORMALITY AND MENTAL HEALTH EMBRACE *(but are not limited to):*

1. A capacity to accept and assume responsibility for oneself.

2. A capacity to be a self-starter—to work on one's own and to work with others.

3. A capacity for spontaneity, wholeheartedness, and commitment.

4. A capacity for appropriate dependency, independence, and/or interdependence.

5. A sense of curiosity and capacity to accept imperfection and incompleteness.

6. A sense of humor and a capacity for playfulness.

7. A capacity to be open to, rather than to deny, the evidence that one's senses perceive.

8. A capacity to be in touch with one's feelings and to take appropriate action in response to what one perceives—while acknowledging that appropriate action at certain times is seeming

inaction and exercising the capacity for "masterful inactivity" or remaining in abeyance until other data dictate that the time is now ripe for action.

9. A minimal tendency to project or externalize responsibility for one's behavior onto others—onto "they" or "them."

10. A capacity for objective awareness as well as for subjective involvement in one's own emotional, psychic, and behavioral functioning.

11. A capacity for objective appraisal as well as for subjective involvement in interpersonal relationships.

12. A capacity (for the most part) to complete tasks voluntarily undertaken.

13. A sufficient degree of tolerance for anxiety to continue functioning in risky and stressful situations and to accept helplessness at times.

14. A capacity to accept and integrate failure, criticism, and rejection.

15. A capacity to take a minority position at times.

16. A capacity to communicate accurately and effectively with others.

17. A capacity to be the prime agent involved in and responsible for the development of one's own potential, and to be motivated more often by one's "wants" than one's "shoulds."

18. A capacity to live with frustration and to postpone "present pleasure" for "future profit" at times.

19. A capacity for satisfaction and joy in some aspects of daily living—at work, at home, or in leisure time activity.

20. Not *expecting* what one only has a right to *hope* for.

21. A capacity to ask, to give, and to receive simply, without strings or reservations.

22. A capacity to live with the ambiguity and paradoxes of life.

23. A capacity for "joie de vivre."

24. A capacity to be open to serendipity—or taking pleasure in unexpected "happenings."

9

Optimal Family Functioning

More or less healthy individuals do not develop by accident. They were raised in family organizations which were more optimal.° Optimal family functioning is based on many factors, including (but not limited to) the following:

1. *Communication is open and direct.* Parents do not talk to each other through the child as conduit nor do they talk about the child in front of him as if he were not present.

2. *The home atmosphere is characterized by a substantial degree of warmth which is experienced overtly as well as covertly.* The family members have a capacity to understand what others are feeling and to communicate it empathetically.

3. *Interest in and caring for one another are expressed behaviorally in touching as well as in words and tone.* It goes from parents to children, children to children, and children to parents and grandparents.

4. *Reaching out to others* is easier for members of healthier families as their basic attitude towards people is one of caring, trusting, and being friendly. In less healthy families there is little or no real caring for, interest in, or trust in each other, usually because of cold home atmosphere with fragmentation of family life. There is a tendency for family members to be isolated, distant, guarded and hostile in their relationships with people outside the family.

5. *Self-perception is more accurate and realistic* in members of healthier families. In dysfunctional (sicker) families, members do not see themselves as others

°A valuable research study and description of what systems and interactions occur in healthier and less healthy families may be found in NO SINGLE THREAD: *Psychological Health in Family Systems* by Jerry M. Lewis, M.D., W. Robert Beavers, M.D., John T. Gossett, Ph.D., and Virginia A. Phillips (Brunner/Mazel, New York, 1976).

see them, tend to deny reality quite often, and have more difficulty in functioning adequately in the world-at-large. (See Chapter 10 page 25 on *Perception* and Chapter 40 page 79 on *Competency in the Art of Daily Living*.)

6. *Expression of emotion is more often positive than negative.* Emotions are acknowledged and not ignored. Anger, sullenness or withdrawal is a sign that something needs to be looked at, more or less changed or corrected. The need for intimacy is respected and fulfilled.

7. *Individuation and autonomy are encouraged,* not just allowed, for each family member, with an appropriate balance between dependency and independence. There is high tolerance and respect for the individual's right to differ verbally (without having to become disagreeable in order to express an opinion or viewpoint) and to be different from other family members in taste or values or behavior so long as it is not destructive to self or others. Self-individuation is enhanced when the right to private thoughts, wishes, feelings, wants, possessions and space for each family member is respected and provided for. Individual members are then more likely to accept responsibility for their own feelings, thoughts and actions.

8. *Power is shared in a good marriage.* Circumstances rather than an arbitrary rigid code decide which marriage partner exerts the greatest influence or power in a given family situation. In a more optimally functioning family, dominance or submission is flexibly expressed. No one member is always dominant or submissive regarding all issues or family tasks; the range of power and its expression is wide. In my opinion, the power operations in most segments of our society at the time of this writing reveal that father still holds the most power, mother holds less power, and the child or children the least power in the family. However, this is currently a controversial issue in family life which is changing in many areas where wives are working outside the home and are bringing in an income sometimes equal to or surpassing the husband's earnings. With the culture-shaking trend we have been experiencing towards women's liberation and equality in the economic world, sports, education, politics, and the military establishment, we are witnessing the struggle of women to equalize housekeeping responsibilities, child-rearing, and the use of power in family life.

As a consequence of these new trends, we are seeing more and more families where power is expressed through a parental coalition which—when respectfully, flexibly and consistently maintained by either or both parents—provides a network of support structures which the child can incorporate into himself and his life with other authorities in the world-at-large as he develops his own potential. As the child experiences and learns to accept the meaning and value, as well as the outer and inner rewards, which accompany his compliance to "Yes" or "No" coming from rational, understandable, consistently evenhanded parental authorities, he is able to feel self-respect and respect for parents and others who offer him appropriate opportunities to be his own authority for himself. He can thus enjoy learning to clarify values for himself and to develop and exercise impulse-control, conscience and a capacity for frustration-tolerance while postponing fulfillment of present wants and gratifications for future value or dividends of one kind or another.

When power is expressed by either or both parents in a rigid, harsh, tyrannical, capricious, inconsistent, and unjust fashion, the child cannot learn to respect authority. He develops inadequate, confused inner authority-structures while building up for immediate or later expression (openly defiant or secretly sabotaging) resentments which are expressed destructively to self or others.

Common familial situations involving abuse of power, which may lead children to compulsive rebellion against authority, as well as to destructive behavior including violence to self or others (animals as well as people) are:

a) When mother, father, both parents or other family members are tyrannical, violent, physically destructive, demeaning, abusive, unjust, capricious, irrational, inconsistent, or not understandable in their expression of power.

b) When one parent and one or more children maintain a collusive alliance to undermine or defeat the potency, authority, wishes, or values of the other parent. For example, in a healthier family a father or mother says, "I feel strongly about this but I will listen to your point of view." In a non-optimally functioning family the father says, "I don't want to hear your comments. When I want them, I'll ask for them! My mind is made up and that's all there is to it. The discussion is over!" He is repeating the old maxims: "Children should be seen and not heard"; "Like dogs, children should be trained to obey!"

9. *Problem-solving is based on an awareness of the complexity of human motivation and functioning.* Problems are identified and approached early. The whole family is more apt to be involved in the search for different options to explain and more effectively cope with individual and family members.

10. *Initiative, spontaneity and assumption of leadership.* Members of more optimally functioning families find it easier to be involved in community, athletic, artistic, educational, and social activites. Dysfunctional family members are often more passive, unimaginative, controlled, and not involved in such outside activities.

11. *The nature and degree of role projection by the parents.* In an optimally functioning family the parents are appropriately, flexibly and adequately present as models to be identified with by children of the same sex.

12. *Sharing of household responsibilities.* There is at least a partial sharing of most, if not all, household responsibilities.

13. *The qualities of satisfaction during parental sexual intercourse.* The greater the degree of satisfaction the more optimal is the quality of the total family life. Frequency of parental sexual intercourse is not as important as satisfaction, intimacy, love, and mutuality.

14. *Parental acceptance.* If at least one parent is strongly accepting, the family may function more optimally. In a family where one parent is rejecting and dominating and the other parent is absent, meek, submissive, or non-supportive, there is much less opportunity for the children to be nurtured towards emotional and attitudinal health. In such families the child's self-image will not be positive and a sense of "belonging" may not develop adequately or even be considered desirable. When parental love is unconditional but acceptance of the child's behavior is conditional, the child may be better equipped for living realistically than if parental love and acceptance of the child's behavior are both unconditional.

15. *The sharing of pain.* In healthier families pain, hurt, sadness, tears, and disappointment are more openly and immediately shared. Multiple kinds and levels of human support can thus be offered to family members who express pain and/or ask for help.

16. *A degree of curiosity and risk-taking* is an important basis for moving out towards others and towards what is new in the world-at-large.

17. *The participation of the parent of the opposite sex in the care and rearing of each child is greater in optimally functioning families.* In families where the father insists that he'll raise the boys and mother can take care of the girls, all the children will grow up with unrealistic perceptions of themselves and their roles as males and females.

18. *Physical contact is frequent, tender, appropriate and non-self-conscious in healthier families.* Males as well as females can hug, kiss and give "strokes" to one another to express warm, loving, accepting, and belonging feelings at times other than crucial "hello's" or "goodbyes." Children raised by parents who rarely or never touched them physically have many problems in accepting closeness and intimacy as adolescents and adults; they often have severe sexual and identity problems as well.

19. *The family's capacity for acceptance of loss.* There is preparation for and acceptance of the separation from the family (as each child grows up and leaves "home") and eventual death of each family member over time. Death is experienced as a reminder of our mortality and a message for us to live as fully and enjoyingly as possible since there seems to be but "one trip around."

20. *The family's perception of reality.* The degree of congruence or harmony between the family's my-

thologies and values and the actual reality of the culture and world of the family will determine whether the child feels more or less comfortable or uncomfortable in the world-at-large. The socially awkward, inept, inadequate, or withdrawn child rarely comes from healthily integrated parents who are socially comfortable and realistic.

21. *A capacity for joy in living (what the French call "joie de vivre").* To the degree that a family is able to enjoy its living and growing together despite economic circumstances and the vicissitudes of life, the individual members of the family can face the fact that life is not easy and can live with hope and optimism rather than hopelessness and despair. Such persons can enjoy what there is to enjoy and accept what needs to be accepted, while using their energies to attempt to change that which needs to be changed.

22. *The capacity for appropriate risk-taking* is higher in an optimally functioning family.

23. *The presence or absence of psychopathology.* The sicker the family, the more likelihood of emotional or mental illness in one or more members. We've learned that often one child becomes the symptom-bearer for the whole family and he or she winds up as the labeled "Patient."

24. *A sense of humor:* in healthier families there is a recognition that all human beings find "it's hard to live," although some find it *easier* than others. It is rarely if ever *easy* to live. This is so for rich and poor, black and white, children, adolescents, adults or the aged. Those who have learned to have a sense of humor about themselves in their family life as they grow up are better equipped to carry that sense of humor into later life.

10

Perception

We usually become aware of patients' *behaviors* before we become aware of how they *perceive*. We've learned that the major point to be noted about patients' behavior is that *it may be more or less inappropriate*. Now let's look at some perceptual functions which are frequently disturbed in people called patients:

1. SENSORY
2. TIME
3. BODY
4. SELF
5. OTHERS
6. THINKING

In reading these comments on perceptions, it is important to keep in mind that patients are often unclear as to the distinction between what originates or goes on inside them and what originates or goes on outside them.

Added to this is the fact that they are plagued with the mental mechanism (see page 129 on mental mechanisms) called projection—*what is inside is experienced as coming from outside*.

Experiencing the world with projection, confusion, and denial leads to a blurring of reality, to further confusion, and then to such difficulties in ordinary daily living that the individual moves towards anger and murderous rage at self and others. The only ways to cope with these feelings, then, may be by withdrawal, acting-out or other bizarre behavior.

What do you see here? Which did you see first, the vase or the faces? Inasmuch as both perceptions are correct this teaches us to be open to the point of view of others.

11

Sensory Perception

Sensory perception usually refers to what is perceived through the five senses—*seeing, hearing, touching, tasting* and *smelling.* One or more of these senses may be blurred, or else heightened and super-clear. This may lead to seeming changes in how people look, what people say or how they feel to us, what food tastes like, awareness of ordinary smells. Visual perspective may be distorted so that depth perception may be lost or the distance between two objects or people may be seen as decreased or increased (*a particularly important factor to keep in mind when you move toward a potentially violent patient; he may overreact if he feels you are getting closer than he feels comfortable with*). A patient's sense of self in space may also be distorted.

Among catatonic patients, at certain times any movement of people may alter what is seen so that the patient stops and stares to create a still rather than a motion picture. If he doesn't move his head or eyes, he is able to see a limited area more clearly. This reduces the anxiety he is filled with as he experiences the world as malevolent.

These altered perceptions of the senses are particularly significant in paranoid and non-paranoid schizophrenics. When accompanied by thought disturbances,

they may lead to non-conforming, oppositional or bizarre behavior. Persons who internally, in their intrapsychic functioning, feel insecure, anxious, and precarious in their "mode-of-being in this world" feel even more precarious when they also have distortions in their sensory perceptions of what is going on in the interpersonal world outside themselves.

Patients diagnosed as schizophrenic often have distortions in their sense of hearing which are called auditory hallucinations. I refer to the process of hearing "voices." These voices may be experienced as:

1. originating in some part of the patient's body;

2. outside voices talking about the patient, frequently making derogatory comments;

3. outside voices talking to the patient and giving orders such as "Hit him," "Push her," "Knock that off the table." These are called "Command Hallucinations";

4. commenting on the patient's thoughts, or repeating his thoughts, or commenting on something the patient is reading.

12

Time Perception

Time perception is often disturbed in psychiatric patients. In the present moment, patients often express a subjective change in how they experience *the flow of time*. A patient may say: "Time dragged when I was a child. I was so bored and depressed most of the time. Now it goes too fast!" "I can't stand free time." "I always leave time to rush." "How could twenty years go by in a day?"

Continuity of time is often disrupted. A person may go through periods of inattentiveness or absenting himself so that he is not consciously aware of or in touch with what is actually going on around him. He may say, "Time has stopped for me." Past, present, and future time awareness may be unrealistically remembered or experienced. There may be a feeling that there is no future. A person may feel he really should have lived in a prior century as he doesn't fit in the present time or generation which moves too fast for him.

In psychiatric hospitals, the following type of dialogue reflecting the blurring of past and present occurs frequently:

Patient to Aide: "My mother just visited me and brought me some cookies."

Therapy Aide to Patient: "It seems to you like it was just now, Harry, but actually your mother visited you yesterday, which was Sunday. And she did bring you cookies, but you ate them with me and the other patients after she left."

Patient to Aide: (looking a little suspicious and confused) "And I was so sure it was just now. It seemed like a few minutes ago. Are you fooling me?"

Time and memory perceptions are closely linked, and the complete evaluation of the mental status of persons who come to psychiatric attention always includes an assessment of their closeness to reality concerning time. Common questions used to establish a basis for evaluation of the patient's time orientation disturbance, if any, are: "What is today's date?" "Do you know what time it is now?" "How long have you been here?" "How old are you?" "When were you born?" "What season is this?" Then the discrepancies, if any, are noted between the patient's responses and your knowledge of his reality.

In patients with senile brain disease and certain other brain disorders, there is a conspicuous disturbance in time and memory perception. Memory for present-time events is markedly absent or distorted in such people, but memory for childhood or early adult life experiences may be accurate.

13

Body Perception

Body perception is commonly distorted or disturbing to our patients. Distortions of the body image usually lead to negative feelings about one's body and to an increase in self-hate or feelings of shame, as well as fear of exposure. For example, a successful, unmarried, good-looking, strong, male college graduate has difficulties over and over again with women. He can't believe they could really love him for anything other than his money. Although he is 34, his body image goes back in time to when he was 10 years old and saw himself as a fat, awkward, lonely and rejected little boy.

Another example is that of a woman of 39 who says, "Very often I'll look at myself in a mirror and be surprised at the facial expression I find there. I know I'm supposed to look like a grown-up woman who is the mother of four children. But my perception is that I'm looking at a girl of 10."

An increase in basic anxiety, a preoccupation with self, and a heightened internal sensory awareness lead to a focus on cardiovascular, respiratory, and gastro-intestinal functioning. Dermatological expression of conflict, anxiety, rage, and confusion may be noted through skin rashes, dermatographia (skin-writing), scratching, and excoriations, especially on hands, face and legs. Some borderline and schizophrenic patients have numerous hypochondriacal symptoms because of their over-focus on and over-concern with their body which parallels the degree of their withdrawal from the world-at-large.

14

Self-Perception

Self-perception refers to how a person is aware of and experiences the many aspects and levels of what goes into his concept of self. There are fixed, rapidly changing and slowly changing aspects in each person's self-perception.

Self-image includes not only what is real and healthy in a person but also what is idealized and potential. It also includes what is hated, despised, to be hidden or gotten rid of in the view of the person called patient. In addition there are all those relatively fixed aspects of self, such as one's name, height, color, body build, sex, language, accent, cultural background, and fixed biological features. Finally, self-image brings together one's general personality features as presented to the world-at-large and one's secret personality features, as well as those personality features which are unknown to self but obvious and visible to others in the form of attitudes and emotional expressions and reactions manifested in behaviors.

In our patients we look for evidence of alienation-from-self, compartmentalizing (when our left hand doesn't know what our right hand is doing), fragmentation of personality, diffusion of identity, dissociation, depersonalization, self-doubt, reduced self-worth/self-esteem, and self-hate in its many forms. We try to reduce the patient's negative self-perception while increasing his positive view of self.

The perceptions persons have of themselves are critical, especially in our assessment of depressed and potentially suicidal patients. For example, a patient who is depressed because of an acute grief reaction and has no energy or desire to get up in the morning to go to work, who has no appetite, and is having difficulty sleeping generally does not present as serious a suicide threat as a patient who feels she is a total failure at everything, feels rejected, friendless and worthless, and feels despicable, ashamed, and full of self-hate because of terrible things she feels, she believes or that she has been told that she has done to others (see page 122 on Suicide).

Our task is to help people develop a better self-concept!

15

Perception Of Others

Perception of others, when accurate, leads a person to the greatest levels of success in interpersonal relationships in daily living. If, however, a person is "allergic" to others because of having suffered numerous severe traumatic early life experiences (put-downs of all types), he will project or transfer or externalize onto others negative, rejecting reactions which he expects from them. He thus manages to create self-fulfilling prophecies of being rejected or victimized no matter how much he has to bend, distort or obliterate reality to do so (see page 55 on redefining people and objects).

Patients have most of their problems in perceiving others accurately when those others are in an authority position with them. They will look for and spot signs of malevolence, unfairness, inconsistency, uncaring, disinterest and dishonesty.

It is our satisfying task to offer them a corrective perceptual and emotional experience by being as honest, non-exploitive, caring, warm, interested, constant, consistent, concerned and simply human as we can be. Such new experiential input from mental health workers may allow for a renewal of trust, hope, intimacy, and positive belief in self which can nurture self-esteem, self-confidence, and a higher degree of inner morale and desire to risk involvement with others—inside and then outside of psychiatric centers.

16

Thought Perception

Thinking is an inner experience whose perception becomes distorted or disturbed:

1. when one's consciousness and brain physiology are altered by drugs (like LSD or marihuana), medications (like barbiturates), or organic disease;

2. more commonly by disorders of the mind and emotions related to one's social existence in the world as we know it.

Thought distortions can be due to inattention, or else can result from absenting oneself from the actual reality one is living in so as to escape into a world of fantasy and imagination.

In psychiatric patients with minor illnesses we can find evidence of distortions in judgment due to an inability to abstract, or to make appropriate connections between past and present events or between a repetitive cause and effect. They just can't seem to mature and learn from past experiences.

In the major psychiatric illnesses referred to as psychotic states we find many more types of thinking—conceptual and perceptual disorders linked together to serve as a basis for inappropriate emotional and behavioral functioning. However, all of these have a circular influence on each other.

Some common thought disorders are:

1. *Difficulties in the associative process.* These result in loose, seemingly extraneous, inappropriate, or disconnected words or thoughts that rush in and interfere with the "thinking-through" of even a minor reality-oriented subject or task. The blockage of such "thinking-through" produces confusion and more disturbance in functioning in simple, everyday living situations because of difficulties in understanding the meaning and logic of situations and words. This then leads to heightened anxiety and fright which are relieved by the person "absenting" himself and withdrawing from other people and situations by moving into a world of fantasy.

Here is an example of loose associations: A 27-year-old, single, intelligent, American-born college drop-out is asked what is troubling him. He responds "I was walking along the street and brown eyes looked at me from behind the post and blinds. There were brown eyes and blue eyes on the steps and I became frightened and went to the policeman. He just laughed at me with his blue eyes. He was part of it. They were out to get me. The machine knew. They were out to get my secret. Brown eyes and blue eyes, brown eyes and blue eyes. I can't talk to you cause you are in with them. Your tie. Brown eyes. You're their agent. I know who you are."

In this example of loose associations we see evidence of ideas of reference—being singled out to be looked at, spied on and persecuted by "others"—which have a grandiose basis. We see the underlying fear of others and the indication of belief in a plot against him. We see the evidence of a secret and the fear that it will be found out. Quite often such a secret relates to something sexual. We see inferences and implications but the referents implied are not made clear. There is a confused, fuzzy, oblique aspect to the whole dialogue and yet there is some clarity too.

Bleuler believed that the loosening of associations was the major mechanism underlying all of the schizophrenic's symptoms. He stated, "the loosening of the associations results in the opening up of wrong pathways of thought, pathways deviating from experience, and on the other hand, the patient is forced to operate with fragments of ideas. The latter abnormality leads to displacements, condensations, confusion, generalizations, clang-associations, illogical thinking and incoherence." He also said, "In schizophrenia, the habitual well-worn pathways of association have lost their cohesiveness. . . . Often enough, instead of by ideas and concepts, the train of thought is determined by mere fragments of such ideas, or by incorrectly combined fragments."°

2. *Delusions* (false beliefs not based on reality)—*often of a persecutory or grandiose nature.*

   (a) *"Ideas of Reference"* commonly occur with delusional perceptions. A patient may think and then believe that newspaper articles or headlines, or the comments made on radio programs, or by the visually experienced television announcer who looks at the viewer in a direct eye-to-eye fashion are sending a message specifically directed to him as part of a larger national or worldwide scheme or plot against him.

   (b) Disturbances such as *thought control* and *thought withdrawal.* Patients may complain that they are being forced to think other people's thoughts, which are very troublesome to them. These thoughts may often be of a sexual nature having to do with incestuous, perverse, bizarre, or immoral behavior. They may also complain that they feel a sensation of thought withdrawal during which they can feel other people or strange

°See E. Bleuler, *Dementia Praecox or The Group of Schizophrenias,* International Universities Press, New York, 1952, pp. 354, 355.

forces taking their own thoughts out of their mind and replacing these thoughts with other thoughts.

(c) The *broadcasting of thoughts* is another phenomenen seen in some psychotic patients. They believe their thoughts are being broadcast to others and so they might say to you: "You know what I'm thinking, so why do you ask what's going on inside of me? You and the others here are tuned in on me all the time through all the electric fixtures, television and radio sets around here."

In (a), (b) and (c) we observe that the basic feeling of inferiority and/or insignificance of the patient is overcompensated for by making self-referenced interpretations of everyday life phenomena which are grandiose and unrealistic.

17 Signs That One Is Moving Toward Mental Illness

1. A degree of prolonged, constant *anxiety, apprehension or fear* which is *not* proportionate with reality. The object or so-called cause of the anxiety may shift from one cause or source to another.

2. The kind of *depression* which is heavy, gnawing, and accompanied by growing inertia and withdrawal from friends or activities, while the person may become apathetic and still or show excessive agitation.°

3. *An abrupt change* in a person's mood or behavior so that his/her relatives, friends, and fellow workers are saying, "He's just not himself anymore. Something's come over him." For example, a formerly cautious and prudent person may suddenly become reckless and seem to squander his money or spend it unwisely. Or a person who was very reliable and considerate now becomes unreliable, self-preoccupied, and inconsiderate of others. Or there may be a rapid change in a person's public sexual behaviors so that they seem bizarre.

4. *Sleep disturbances*—sleeping too much; not sleeping enough; trouble falling asleep and then being unable to get up in the morning; trouble staying asleep; restless or nightmarish sleep; getting up too early and being unable to fall asleep again; staying awake all night and sleeping all day.

5. *Appetite disturbances*
   (a) *Eating*—loss of appetite with loss of weight; gain of weight due to excessive eating; bizarre tastes in eating which suddenly develop, such as a paranoid patient who will suddenly refuse to eat certain types of foods because he believes that these are poisoned.
   (b) *Drinking*—excessive intake of fluids of all kinds; drinking too many alcoholic beverages of any kind or mixture.

6. *Disturbances in Sexual Functioning*
   (a) A loss of sexual drive or interest.

°The recent movie "A Woman Under The Influence" provides an excellent portrayal of a woman moving downhill toward mental illness as well as providing us with a picture of the family factors contributing to the development of her illness.

(b) A sense of disgust, dirtiness, or shame associated with sexual organs or sexual activity. Such persons become unusually prim, proper, and righteous.

(c) Premature ejaculation.

(d) Inability by male or female to have orgasm despite prior freedom to "let go."

(e) A desire to mutilate or amputate one's sexual organs.

(f) A preoccupation with sex and sexual organs.

(g) An obsession with the idea of exposing one's sexual organs.

(h) A compulsion to actually expose oneself which can no longer be inhibited. A woman's blouse may be unbuttoned or she may sit with legs wide apart though wearing a skirt. A man may walk around with his pants unzippered.

(i) The development of phobias which are related to exaggerated sexual feelings, including a strong fear of being raped.

(j) Promiscuity.

(k) Sexual recklessness.

(l) Heightened fear of homosexuality.

(m) A woman who formerly enjoyed vaginal intercourse with her husband may begin to complain of pain on penetration and avoid sexual activity with him. Commonly, in the absence of a physical cause the basis for the change is her deep-seated anger at him which she is unaware of or unable to express because of fear of abandonment.

18

Assessing a Patient

The rapid assessment of a mental patient is not necessarily accomplished by asking a series of mechanized routine questions. Formerly, we would ask such questions as "Do you know where you are? Do you know what day this is? Do you know who is the President of the United States? Who was President before him? Do you know my name?"

Although there is a value in routinely asking certain questions in order to check the patient's orientation and memory, some of us attempt to establish a free flowing exchange of dialogue between the patient and ourselves. It starts with where we are now—meaning the context or background of the setting in which we meet. If the patient is sitting at a lunch table, I might ask if he's enjoying or has enjoyed the food here. If he's sitting watching a television show, I might ask him if it's a good show or how much he's enjoying it. If he's seated on a bench outside his inpatient unit reading a magazine, I might greet him with a remark about what a pleasant day it is and then inquire as to what he's reading. There is value in creat-

ing a personal conversational bridge which has "here-and-now" relevance.

Whatever I approach the patient with *from the point of view of content* provides an opportunity *from the point of view of process* to observe and make inferences about him from his nonverbal behaviors and responses as well as from his verbal content. I can immediately sense his attitude from his manner of responding and I can tell by his responses what he thinks of me and my move toward him.

Is he welcoming or rejecting? While I introduce myself by name, does he respond to my hand extended for a handshake with his own hand extended to me in a warm or welcome or shy or frightened or anxious manner, or not at all? Does he appear apprehensive about my asking to join him or is he pleased?

Are his responses to the situation appropriate or inappropriate? How about my responses? Are they appropriate and authentic, or phony and a put-on which is patronizing or demeaning? Am I aware that he is assessing me to determine how real I am and whether I can be trusted?

19

The First
Three Minutes

The crucial three minutes

The first 3 minutes are crucial in assessing where and how the patient is.

They can reveal:

1. Attitude.

2. Mood or emotion, and its constancy or rapidity of change.

3. Intellectual state.

4. Contact with reality.

5. Relationship with interviewer.

6. Degree of voluntary cooperation or lack of it.

7. Memory.

8. Alertness or degree of being drowsy or confused because of:
—psychiatric disturbance;
—medication (large dose of major tranquilizer);
—alcohol;
—other toxic substances (reefers, LSD, etc.);
—physical disability
   due to an illness such as a "stroke" (cerebral hemorrhage);
   due to aging that produces senile brain disease.

9. Behavior.

10. Whether I like this patient or not.

11. Whether I'm comfortable with this patient or not.

20 Highlights Of Here-and-Now Observations

Intellectual Functioning

Clear/Alert ↔ Foggy/Clouded/Confused.

Understands Easily ↔ Great Difficulty in Understanding. (Is it due to low I.Q. or to language difficulty?)

Stream of Mental Activity Is Disordered—word salad, flight of ideas, neologisms (new words), repetitive, talks in jingles.

Overproductive—runs on and on and rambles.

Underproductive—little or no speech while sitting or standing in fixed position.

Thought Content indicates Delusions/Hallucinations

Orientation or Disorientation for
TIME (Present time, day, month, year?)
PLACE (Where are we now? home? hospital? school? police station?)
PERSON (Who are you? Who am I? Who are members of your family?)

Memory for Present, Recent and Past—all intact? some intact? which are disturbed?

Intelligence—Educational background?
I.Q.? Capacity for abstraction? Comprehension?

Attention Span

Degree of Insight and Judgment Concerning Self and
Others—Understands and accepts need for treatment
or denies it.

Behavioral Reactions

Attitude—Cooperative/Helpful/Interested.
—Uncooperative/Resistive.
—Indifferent.

Behavior—is controlled.
—is uncontrolled with ward staff? doctors? other patients? relatives?

Coordination and Gait Normal or Disturbed? How?

Distrusting/withdraws/isolates self into corner of room
or into a room by self. Rarely talks to or has contact
with anyone.

Shy/Meek/Introverted—Self effacing/Appeasing.

Pushy/Aggressive/Extroverted.

Seductive/Dramatic/Hysterical.

Resigned.

Psychomotor Retardation (sluggishness) all the way to
mute—or Agitation (restlessness/inability to sit or
stand still/fast talking/hyperactivity).

Passive-Aggressive—Superficially compliant but actually aggressively thwarting.

Destructive
    To Self—makes suicidal attempts; picks at skin,
    making excoriations; bites nails, fingers, lips.
    To Others—assaultive, hits, spits, abuses, kicks,
    shoves, throws things.

Regressive—doesn't control urine or bowel movements, eating habits sloppy, thickened speech.

Personal Appearance
Shows average concern; little or no concern (doesn't wash or bathe voluntarily, dirty clothes, slovenly, unkempt, unshaven, no make-up); too much concern —excessive or bizarre make-up.

Emotional Reactions

General Mood is:
Average—normal and appropriate in this situation.
Adaptive or high/elated/euphoric/manicky/expansive.
Low—depressed/sad/tearful.

Volatile—quickly springs from one emotion to another (to be distinguished from hysterical°).

Helpful/Motivated.

Caring/Protective.

Open and Receptive to Closed.

Suspicious—shows in manner and eyes.

Irritable—annoyed/angry/enraged.

Enraged to Murderous.

°Chodoff and Lyons defined "the hysterical personality" as "persons who are vain and egocentric, who display labile and excitable but shallow affectivity, whose dramatic, attention-seeking and histrionic behavior may go to the extremes of lying and even pseudological phantastica (an elaborate fantasy construction), who are very conscious of sex, sexually provocative yet frigid and who are dependently demanding in interpersonal relationships" ("Hysteria, the hysterical personality and hysterical conversion," *American Journal of Psychiatry,* 114:734-746, 1958). In working with patients who have established lifelong oppositional or adversarial relationships with themselves and the world of people they come in contact with, it is best to create modest goals to strive towards rather than optimal goals which are hardly likely to be achieved.

Bitter to Vindictive.

Bullying.

Negativistic.

Oppositional to Belligerent.

Uncaring.

Anxious/Fearful/Apprehensive/On-the-verge-of-panic.

Remorseful/Guiltridden.

Ingratiating.

Playful/Kittenish/Joyful.

Affectionate—sensual/sexual.

Appealing to Unappealing.

Judgmental to Righteous.

Abused.

Neutral, Weighing, Reserving Judgment.

Masked, Unfathomable.

Vacant, Spiritless.

21

Notes
On Diagnosis

The tentative diagnosis made when the patient is first admitted to an inpatient unit is not necessarily the final diagnosis. It may change rapidly as the patient's condition changes from initial confusion, general recalcitrance, uncooperativeness, and pugnacity. Hopefully, he is helped to move toward clarity, some insight as to "why" he is in the hospital, and a state of cooperative, non-belligerent (although sometimes reluctant) acceptance of his need for temporary hospitalization. We must not continue to look at the patient with "old eyes" (as he was at the moment he was admitted), but rather see him daily with openness and "new eyes."

When a person is most acutely disturbed and psychotic it may be very difficult to decide if he is in the throes of a manic-depressive-manic episode, acute schizophrenia, a toxic or an organic psychotic state. What is most helpful is to obtain an accurate and thorough history. Has he been ill this way before? When? How often? With what precipitating factors? Is there a family history of mental illness? Of psychiatric hospitalization? Of symptoms similar to those of the patient? At what age? In which member(s) of the family? For how many generations? With the answers to these and other related questions, it will be much easier to make an accurate diagnosis and establish an appropriate treatment plan.

The "diagnosis" is actually an ongoing process (not a fixed entity) and should reflect the daily changes in the patient's emotional, psychic, and behavioral condition. Patients should be given opportunities for self-expression, self-government, self-choice, and self-responsibility as soon as they show they can handle these to an increasing degree each day.

The patient is a changing battle-ground of inner and outer personal conflicts and his healthy constructive potentials and forces are constantly attempting to assert themselves over restrictive, crippling, and tyrannical inner neurotic and psychotic forces, as well as outer tyrannical, non-equalitarian, non-nurturing forces in his environment, whether they be in the hospital, at home, or on the street.

Look for and address what is healthier in your patient and you'll see how much better is your developing relationship!

22   Ways To Inspire Hope and Trust In Treatment

Your approach needs to be "hand-tailored" for each individual when you approach acutely ill patients or chronic patients. You must *communicate to each patient that you care* enough for or about him or her to make efforts to help.

Help patients understand that *they can (more or less) expect to improve and get better.* But it is a two-way street. That is, *if they will cooperate with the treatment plan* worked out individually for them by the treatment team, then they can look forward to feeling better inside themselves and about themselves, and they can learn to get along better with other people.

Help patients understand that changing and improving involves *work by* and *with* and *on themselves,* and not just by the staff. Real treatment occurs when patients get involved in their own treatment. They must be encouraged to wholeheartedly participate in the entire program personally designed for them. They must be encouraged to speak up openly at therapy sessions, especially in group therapy and therapeutic community meetings, or at patient government meetings; to express their opinions about what is going on in their daily life in the hospital or their daily life as outpatients; to talk about what goes on during the evening and during the night as well as in the daytime and on weekends. Weekends and nights, when most structured activities are suspended, are the times when crises frequently develop. A patient is more likely to trust your movements toward him when he realizes your interest encompasses all 24 hours of his daily life.

Point out and emphasize over and over again that *in developing competency and adequacy* as persons in their life in the hospital, they are preparing themselves to participate more efficiently and with more satisfaction in their family, working, or leisure life outside the hospital. Be inspirational and hopeful. Inspire patients to believe they can develop a healthier, happier, and more decent life for themselves.

43

23

Empathy

To me, empathy means an insightful, subjective, non-critical awareness of the feelings, emotions and what is going on inside another person.°

The capacity to relate empathetically is a major attribute of successful mental health workers. An effective, helping person communicates in a non-defensive, non-phony, genuine way through multiple levels and multiple channels the fact that he is accepting, that he feels a non-possessive warmth for and interest in the patient or client, and that he is making a sincere effort to see and understand the world from the other person's point of view. *"I am trying to see what you perceive as you see it from inside you."*

An effective helping person communicates a high degree of empathetic understanding which, in effect, says to the patient or client: *"I am trying to really hear and know your problems and your feelings as you are experiencing and perceiving them. I am listening not only to your words with my two ears that you can see, but also with my third and fourth and fifth ears and other senses and ways of knowing you as well. I am here as a whole person who is more than just physically present and I am listening to all of you with all of me as my sensing instrument. I am with you as a person on a moment-to-moment basis and sensitive to your unspoken as well as your spoken utterances as you change from moment to moment, as you move from trusting to not trusting, from security with me to insecurity with me, from being more cooperative to being more resistant and less cooperative."*

When you can clearly grasp the patient's meaning even though she didn't clearly state it with her words, she develops a respect for the quality and depth of your interest, concern, and competency.

°Compassion, sympathy and pity are often confused with empathy. Compassion is a soft, warm, kind feeling for another person whose pain and suffering we can identify with. Sympathy is a feeling of kindly resonance towards and with another person. It is similar to but not exactly the same as compassion. Pity is different from empathy, compassion and sympathy in that it is not usually welcomed by healthier self-respecting individuals because it implies the person who does the pitying is on a higher or more adequate level than he or she who is the "object" of the pity. Some people say, "I would rather be scorned than pitied."

She may remark with pleased surprise, "You understand just what I'm feeling. You're different from the other people I've talked to." That may be her way of recognizing and accepting that *you are with her!*

Your empathetic interest and understanding may be communicated when you offer a tentative suggestion as to something the patient may be feeling and the patient may then say, "Yes, that's right. I'm clearer about it now."

When the other person has real trouble in expressing what he or she is feeling or thinking, I find it of value to guide the person towards words or pictures to describe what's going on inside by asking, *"It's as if what? As if what is going on inside you?"* I offer the option to describe the indescribable with metaphors or other universal human experiences which we both have known and thus can bridge the space between us. It is this type of simple intervention which not only improves communication and understanding but also conveys to the other person that "I'm With You!"

In training mental health workers to be more capable of empathizing with patients and their families the focus shifts from "what did you see?" to "what did you feel?" to "what were the patient and his family experiencing?"*

* H. L. Muslin and N. Schlessinger, "Toward the Teaching and Learning of Empathy," *Bulletin of the Menninger Clinic*, 35: 262-271, 1971.

24

Communicating "I'm With You"

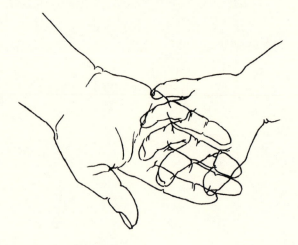

In order for us to provide services for and work helpfully with people called patients, each of us has to communicate that "I'm with you."° What we do to demonstrate this is:

1. We move *toward patients*—to join them where they are and *not expect them* to be where we are.

2. We are understanding of *where they are.*

3. We are *constructive* in what we say and do.

°See film series entitled "Working With People Called Patients" produced in 1975 at South Beach Psychiatric Center.

Part I: "I'm with You" on 30 min. 16 mm. black and white sound movie or videotape cassette.

Part II: "Tuning In" on 30 min. 16 mm. black and white sound movie or videotape cassette.

Write to: South Beach Education, Training and Research Fund, 777 Seaview Avenue, Staten Island, N.Y. 10305 for rental or purchase information.

4. We are *compassionate.*

5. We *build* self-esteem and self-confidence and do all we can to *reduce their self-hate.*

Here are some ways we show or say "I'm with you."

1. By showing *interest.*

2. By asking the right questions, such as: *"What* is going on in you?" *"What* went on in you at that moment?" rather than *"Why* did you do that?" *"Why* did you say that?" "Didn't you know it was a *stupid* thing to say?"

3. By expressing *concern* and *caring.*

4. By *accepting* the patient where and how he is based on where he's come from, but having in mind the possibility of his changing—without condemning him.

5. By being *respectful.*

6. By being *real* and *aware.*

7. By *inspiring trust and hope.*

8. By *clarifying* and *educating* patients as to what life really is about—painful as well as potentially joyous for all, not just for him; frustrating and not just gratifying for all—not just for him; that none of us can expect what we only have a right to hope for.

9. By *suggesting new options,* alternatives or solutions.

10. By being *sensitive to boundaries and limitations*—physical, spatial, emotional, cultural, etc.

11. By pointing out how *a glass* can be seen as *half full* as well as half empty. If the patient will look at the same data differently and more positively, he can thus learn to see and appreciate what he has in the way of *resources and assets* rather than focusing on his liabilities and on what he doesn't have.

12. By *being hopeful* despite the difficulties in the situation.

13. By expressing a sense of *"humor."*

14. By helping him to see that in view of his life history and background he may have done *the best he could with what he's got*—so far—but implying he might be able to do more with his assets in the future if he doesn't give up.

25

Pro-therapeutic Attitudes

Develop attitudes expressing your:

Concern for patient's safety and wellbeing.

Interest.

Readiness to be of help.

Capacity for caring and constancy.

Attentiveness.

Understanding.

Support for and encouragement of his efforts.

Expression of trust in the patient and his potentials.

Hopefulness about his "making it."

Respect for the patient as a person with human rights (see page 132 for detailed statement on patient's rights).

Respect for the patient's accomplishments.

Interest in his/her potential for developing his strengths, skills, latent resources, talents and gifts.

Respect for the patient's efforts even when he continues to fail or is awkward or inept.

Respect for his having suffered but not rewarding him for suffering. (Too many patients have been led to believe that "Life owes me a living and a loving because I've suffered so much.")

Empathic acceptance of his situation.

Pro-therapeutic attitudes are conveyed in common statements like:

"You're doing better with that today"

"I like the way you look today"

"Your enthusiasm is catching. May we join you?"

"That's beautiful. Would you share some with me?"

26

Anti-therapeutic Attitudes

By anti-therapeutic, we mean such attitudes as:

Ignoring patients.

Treating patients as if they were objects or numbers.

Being disrespectful of patients' basic human rights.

Not listening to patients.

Pushing or herding patients like sheep or other animals.

Demeaning, discounting, or otherwise belittling patients.

Hassling.

Teasing.

Treating patients continuously like children.

Guilt-provoking.

Shaming, mocking, or ridiculing patients.

Exploiting patients.

Misusing patients sexually.

Displacing your angry and violent feelings onto patients.

Anti-therapeutic attitudes are often conveyed in common statements which are experienced as "put-downs":

"Can't you ever do things right?"

"Is it that hard to make it on time?"

"Do you think I have nothing else to do but pick up after you?"

"Look how dirty you are! Can't you keep yourself clean?"

"Can't you say thank you?"

"Do you think you're at the Waldorf?"

"Don't ask any questions, just do as I tell you."

27 Psychotherapy— What Is It All About?

Though historically referred to as the "Talking Cure," it IS a lot more than just talk.

It is a *system* composed of various *theories—*
and *techniques* or *behaviors*
and *interventions*
and *interpretations*
and *communicating*
and *relating*

which serve the best interests of patients of all types in all settings

by

Exposing	Mixing
Exploring	Uniting
Experiencing	Integrating

origins, meaning and values of
   inner thoughts
   feelings
   reactions
   wishes
   drives
   wants
	conscious and unconscious
	concrete and abstract
	feeling and thought and behavior
	body and mind and environment
	specific and general
	individual and universal
	earthbound (everyday) and
	mystical (ideal and fantasized)
		personal and impersonal
		subjective and objective
		everyday and the unusual
		past and in the present
		realistic with unrealistic
		rational and irrational

as well as

What is not yet considered rational or irrational although it is perceived, experienced as "being," and involved in "becoming" . . .

All this is hopefully to bring about insight, understanding and *change*

Psychotherapists with different theoretical training achieve similar results. Success seems to be more dependent on their active, hopeful, interested, and wholehearted personality than on the intellectual wisdom of their questions, interpretations or other comments. The devices or tools used by most therapists are: (1) the taking of a detailed history and open review of it with the patient; (2) teaching patients to express, listen to and use their "free-associations"; (3) attending to and focusing the patient's interest on context of, free associations to and possible implications of "slips-of-the-tongue"; (4) focusing on shifts from "I" to "you" or to generalities like "one usually feels this way, doesn't everyone?"; (5) interesting patients in recalling and examining their dreams, fantasies and daydreams; (6) focusing on evidence of Idealized Images of Self and their handmaiden which is Self-Hate for not living up to their idealized image; (7) projective techniques, including psychological tests, drawings, directed-fantasies; (8) looking for covert, hidden or unconscious implications in manifest and conscious content; (9) attending to and looking for the meanings of nonverbal behaviors especially when these nonverbal behaviors contradict what's said verbally; (10) focusing on "blind spots," denials and projections; (11) looking for the patient's repeated role in bringing on his own self-defeating patterns and systems and helping him to find new options by giving up old systems and scripts and injunctions; (12) focusing on assets and resources and encouraging their development.

Awareness is a stepping stone to collecting knowledge. When this knowledge is integrated and moved into appropriate action, we are on the road to wisdom and real self-fulfillment.

28 Famous Last Words Used To Ward Off Change

Despite their pain and cry for help, some people unwittingly and unconsciously block or automatically resist the help offered to them. The following phrases are commonly used and serve as clues to such resistance to change. They must be heard and then repeated and examined to root out the underlying hopelessness or feeling of "I can't change."

"By the way . . ."

"If only I were stronger . . ."

"If only I were more of a man . . ."

"If only I were more of a woman . . ."

"If only I showed my anger . . ."

"If only I had spoken up . . ."

"It was all right . . . but it wasn't great!"

"No . . . but . . ."

"Yes . . . but . . ."

"I don't know why but . . ."

"I'm more aware of it now though . . ."

"I realize that but . . ."

"Yes, you're right . . . but you should have seen how I was before!"

"Not too much . . ."

"Not too bad . . ."

"Well—I kind of enjoyed it a little . . ."

"I can't."

"I couldn't care less . . ."

"You're wrong. I tried that and it doesn't help."

"Well, to be perfectly honest with you! . . ."

"But it's not easy . . ."

"But you sound like you think I do it on purpose . . ."

"I know, but I didn't know any better."

"Well . . . not really . . ."

"Well, I'll work on it on my own . . ."

"But it isn't fair . . ."

"Do you think I like being this way?"

"I know but . . ."

"Well, anyway—like I was saying . . ."

"But you don't understand . . ."

"I tried that one but . . ."

"I like to work on it on the outside—on my own!"

"I couldn't help it . . ."

"If you only knew what I went through, you'd
    realize . . ."

"I . . . don't know"

"But I don't know how to change."

"But I don't know where to begin."

"I can't be bothered . . ."

"Yes . . . but isn't that your responsibility. After all,
    you're the therapist . . ."

"I don't remember . . ."

"That's true! But what have you done for me lately?"

"You don't really care about me . . . 'cause if you did then
    you'd . . ."

"I'm sorry . . ."

"I want what I want when I want it!"

"But why didn't you tell this to me sooner?"

"Leave me alone . . ."

"But aren't we all? . . . (or "isn't everybody?")

"I agree . . . but . . ."

29 Can We Reach Schizophrenic Patients?

Yes! We can do psychotherapeutic and counseling work with patients suffering from the schizophrenic syndrome. Is it enough to say that those people called schizophrenic have a split personality? No! In our society we are all split and pushed and pulled in many ways. What is it then? Well . . .

Schizophrenia is a term describing a large group of symptoms or disorders of psychotic dimension manifested by characteristic disturbances of thought, mood and behavior.

Thought disturbances frequently involve abstraction, concept formations, and perception of time, place, and person with ideas of reference, suspicion, fear, and dissociations leading to delusions and hallucinations which are frequently persecutory or grandiose.

Mood disturbances include ambivalence, shallow and inappropriate affects, emotional excitement and turmoil, depression, mania, mutism, and fear leading to panic at times.

Behavior disturbances may include withdrawal, regression, bizarre mannerisms, negativism, excitement, and violence.

Patients with acute schizophrenic episodes have a better prognosis than those whose manifestations are of a chronic debilitating or deteriorating nature. Diagnosis must include consideration of genetic, endocrine, medical, psychological, and socioeconomic stress factors, and treatment may involve psychopharmacological, psychotherepeutic and socioenvironmental approaches.

Regardless of the type of schizophrenic diagnosis, the basic principles of working with people called patients are the same!

It has been said that there are as many individual forms of the schizophrenic syndrome as there are persons suffering from it. And the same holds true for persons caught up in any of the psychoneurotic syndromes.

In working with schizophrenic patients and many others as well:

1. *The therapist must be more active and must repeatedly reach out towards the patient.* There is no room here for super-sensitive, "hurt" feelings on the part of the therapist. He must declare who he is in a realistic manner, but must not guilt-

provoke the patient who has already experienced a lifetime of that with significant others.

2. *The therapist must extend himself in ways which can nurture a healthier ego or feeling of self in the patient*—offering what is a new experience for the patient, an experience in which trust, mutuality, human warmth, congruency, and regard have the highest value.

3. *The therapist's openness with himself, his feelings, and inner experience* provides a model for the patient whom he can emulate or incorporate. The patient can then be encouraged to risk exposing himself to what he has found to be threatening in his previous human relationships.

Schizophrenic patients, like so many others who are not quite as disabled psychiatrically, are bombarded daily with a tremendous "push-pull" conflict — described by Gibson° as their "need-fear dilemma." They need other people desperately to shore up their own inadequate, weak sense of "self," and yet at the very same moment find themselves desperately threatened by this other person whom they are dependent upon. Such persons have difficulty in relating with other people because: they find it hard to organize, control, and maintain their own management decisions and functions, that is, their own healthy self-government operations; they find it hard to maintain a clear picture of what is going on inside and outside themselves and therefore have numerous problems in functioning with others on a reality-based level.

The more precarious, insecure, and frightening the position he finds himself in, the more dependent the patient becomes; the more dependent he now becomes, the more precarious, insecure, isolated, and frightening is the position he finds himself in.

Patients now try to adopt three major patterns in their attempt to reconstitute themselves and their environment:

1. *They may cling to other people* to gain support of an auxiliary ego or self vicariously or through symbiosis, *as if* borrowing or incorporating the strengths of the other person.

2. *They may avoid other people* to escape their fear of being controlled or engulfed or taken over by the other person. This is a basis for much of the withdrawal they manifest.

3. *They may attempt to redefine the other person* so that certain qualities of that person which they need to perceive are built in or retained, and certain qualities of that other person which may induce fear are not perceived or experienced.

Here is an example of the background and present functioning of a 36-year-old, unmarried, American-born man raised by a very old, dominated, mostly absentee father and an overprotective, very old, demeaning, suspicious mother who sent him thousands of contemptuous messages telling him that he was too inadequate and weak to make it in life like other "boys." His self-image is that of a young, weak boy who believes he is not very masculine.

°Gibson, Robert W. "The Hospital Treatment of the Schizophrenic Syndrome; The Role of Object Relations", Chapter 10, pages 110-120 in *The Schizophrenic Reactions: A Critique of the Concept, Hospital Treatment, and Current Research*, ed. by Robert Cancro, Brunner Mazel, New York 1970.

When he is most anxious, he believes he hears different voices in different places calling him "Nanny." He tends to avoid people as he believes himself to be a "creep," and after a few drinks at a bar tends to look and act aggressively to prove his manliness; he has almost gotten himself into serious brawls on a number of such occasions. He states, "There is a clear-cut connection between my fear, my womanish feelings, and talking. When I feel these feelings, I go into a store and stand for a long time looking at the clerk, afraid to talk to him to ask for what I want —feeling like a child at his mercy."

"On another occasion," he recalled, "I returned from the barber shop and told my mother I'd been talking with the barber. She then told me it was dangerous to say where I lived or to give off any information as I might get kidnapped."

This man's programmed fearfulness and suspicious nature made him look for malevolence in all directions, and he had much difficulty in believing that anyone could love or accept him and believe he was "OK." He would constantly look a situation over to find evidence of being "put-on" or "put-down." A typical example of his multiple perceptual distortions was this: "When I was about nine years old, an old man, Mr. Saunders, was visiting at our home and later got into our car to go somewhere with us. He wore a stone in his tie which I thought might be a gallstone he'd had removed in an operation. In the car I turned around repeatedly to look at him and the stone in his tie, and I burst out crying. He looked evil to me. And I put the same symbolism of evil on the spoke wheels of my dead grandfather's touring car and on my father's horn-rimmed glasses."

In this example we find repeated evidence of a person who has from an early age redefined people and other objects in such a fashion that his basic anxieties,

fears, and insecurities have a seemingly real or "rational" basis in the data he perceives. It is of great importance that we attempt to find the basis for the patient's beliefs or conclusions *from his point of view.* What may seem partially or completely irrational or delusional to us may seem rational and realistic to the patient. *We must develop the capacity to identify with the patient and with what is going on inside of him, while simultaneously maintaining our own objectivity.* If the patient can feel our sincerity in attempting to understand his situation from *his point of view,* he may then become open to us and trusting enough to attempt to see the same situation from *our point of view.* In that lies hope for change and a way out of his fearful dilemma.

This pattern of redefining other people and things is a major pseudo-solution (not a real solution) to the inner terror and other fragmentation experienced inside the schizophrenic person. The system of redefining his environment is supported by and rendered easier by his capacity to distort what he or she perceives through the ordinary senses of hearing, seeing, touching, tasting, and smelling—as well as through his capacity for imagining. The distortions are based on each individual's past traumatic experiences. When a schizophrenic patient creates a grandiose delusion and tells you that he is God or the President, he redefines his position of feeling powerless to that of feeling powerful. And at the very same moment and with the very same delusion he redefines your position of being powerful (as he perceives it) and renders you less powerful than himself. Perhaps he can even vengefully create in you some of the helpless feelings he so often feels in your hands. This vindictive triumph, begun with a thought, may serve to dispel some of the tremendous anger and murderous rage which so often accompany his helplessness and which his healthier self is so often afraid will erupt out of control. He thus controls others and his environment with his grandiose delusions, just as he makes himself a continued victim and miserable with his delusions of persecution which may stimulate your compassion, your concern, and your need or desire to help him.

These patterns or sub-systems of clinging, avoiding, or redefining are not consistent, and usually shift very rapidly, leading to that degree of confusion and helplessness in the helper which is so common in our work with such patients. If we can become clear about these elusive patterns which are like shifting sands, we can maintain a measure of steadfastness in our interest, care, concern, and warmth which serves as an increasingly important anchorage for the torn, frightened, shifting patient who lives with a feeling of being anxious, helpless, weak, and isolated in the face of a hostile world.

Mental health workers, professionals as well as paraprofessionals, are extremely dedicated in their concern to care for and "heal" the mentally disturbed. Often they are driven by an unconscious "rescue fantasy" stemming from their own early family life. It is most important that they do not become so involved with an inflated belief in their ability that they go into depression with a deep sense of personal failure when they experience their inadequacy in working with schizophrenic or other patients.

30 Approaching Paranoid Patients

The term "paranoid" is used not only by mental health workers but also very loosely by the public-at-large. In psychiatry, we usually use this term to refer to individuals who are reacting irrationally in believing that people are plotting, scheming, or otherwise engaged in persecuting them. In order to have a basis for their feeling-thought reaction, they project their suspicions to others, have many ideas-of-reference (experiencing the television announcer as sending a special message to them), and distort reality as well as create delusions and hallucinations of a persecutory and gradiose nature (see page 32).

In everyday life, people who are experienced as rejection-collectors or who always wind up feeling they are victimized by others are referred to loosely by others as "paranoid," i.e., believing people are against them.

To establish a relationship with a paranoid patient, it is most important to cultivate the art of listening with respect, interest, and varying degrees of non-judgmental detachment, while not communicating facially your skepticism or disbelief in the patient's delusions. It is most important that whatever you say is honest, though you do not have to state everything going on inside you. Paranoid patients watch your every move, listen carefully to what you say, and remember things you may have forgotten. Therefore, it is crucial to establish a trusting relationship, if it is at all possible, by evidencing your reliability, consistency, and integrity whenever possible.

Polatin emphasizes the point that, "The patient must be brought to see the therapist as a neutral person who does not condemn, depreciate or reject the patient's ideas; the patient thus can be encouraged to break through his isolation and communicate to the therapist his frightening experiences, knowing that he will not take sides. Once this relationship is established, with good communication and trust in the therapist, the latter may offer tentative and alternative speculations concerning factors entering into the delusional picture, so that the patient begins to catch glimpses of his world from another's point of view. In this manner, doubts may arise in the patient's mind concerning the validity of his own assumptions, and the beginning of a more realistic self-appraisal in relation to present reality may develop."[*]

Clinicians who have worked successfully with paranoid patients have found that it takes the building up of a sound, reliable, trusting, and accepting relationship with another person to serve as a basis for the patient to seriously consider giving up his suspicious, self-defeating worldview in favor of the other person's.

A 40-year-old sensitive, intelligent man who had suffered a number of paranoid episodes of different durations stated: "What was the most helpful to me was the therapist's 'friendliness and no bullshitness.' When the therapist looked at me in a friendly way and the other members in my group were friendly then I'd feel that this is the way people relate and I'd go outside therapy and find that people were friendly there too, because I expected them to be that way. By 'no bullshitness' I mean the therapist didn't try to act, but was there as himself with a sense of integrity and a sense of reality. No games were being played. I felt the therapist's straightness also in his wanting me to be straight and level with him and not to play silly games."

[*]Polatin, P., *A Guide to Treatment in Psychiatry*, Philadelphia; Lippincott, 1966, p. 227.

31 New Medicines For Emotional and Mental Problems

There are many drugs being used in the treatment of emotional and mental problems. They serve as:

TRANQUILIZERS

To reduce painful and crippling anxiety, fear, thoughts, or anger. The major tranquilizers alleviate, reduce, and sometimes remove obsessional and paranoid thoughts, hallucinations, delusions. They may also have a profound sedative effect.

SEDATIVES

To reduce hyperactivity or quiet down excessive nervous system functioning, whether that is producing "stomach butterflies," diarrhea, constipation, hypertension, a feeling of tightness in the head, throat, chest or body as-a-whole, or just plain "nerves."

SLEEP INDUCERS

Often the same chemical as used for daytime sedation, but prescribed in larger amounts. Also, these include specific medications prescribed only at bedtime to aid in falling asleep or staying asleep throughout the night.

ENERGIZERS, STIMULANTS & MOOD ALTERATORS

To relieve depression and make one feel more alive, more energetic, more alert in his or her mental functioning. Some stimulants also serve as appetite reducers. Some are very useful in also getting people to fall asleep and stay asleep.

60

Appetite Reducers

Some new medications serve to reduce the desire for food without excessively stimulating the blood pressure or nervous system.

It is important to be aware that all of these new medicines may have disturbing side effects which have to be looked for by us. Some common side effects are drowsiness, dry mouth, low blood pressure, fibrillations, tremors, and weight gain.

Each time any of these powerful medications is prescribed, we have to consider the drawbacks as well as the advantages of each medicine for each individual patient. While a powerful phenothiazine may be properly prescribed for a violent, delusional patient, who is acting-out command hallucinations, because it will have a sedative as well as an anti-delusional effect, it may be better to use a less sedating, newer, anti-psychotic medicine to relieve the delusions in a withdrawn, mute patient.

The new medicines shorten the stay of patients in the hospital and have been a major factor in the emptying of our public mental hospitals in the last decade. While there is an obviously positive value in reducing hyperactivity and psychotic acting-out in persons destructive to themselves and others, there is, however, the real danger that some patients are being made into "zombies" with doses of tranquilizers which reduce the need for adequate nursing and psychotherapeutic help.

The need for adequate after-care facilities is increased by the discharge of so many formerly unmanageable chronic patients from hospitals into the community. They must not be allowed to simply roam the streets and to give up taking medication until the time they are rehospitalized for aberrant behavior as part of a revolving-door syndrome. This is the "no-man's land" of modern community psychiatry and represents the failure element of an otherwise successful community effort.

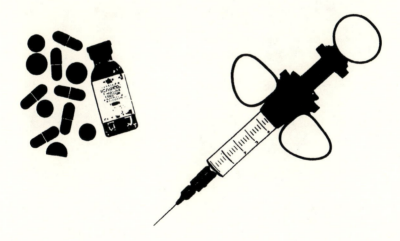

32 Psychiatric Crises and Emergencies

The best way to handle crises and emergencies is to prevent them by recognizing the signs of a developing psychiatric crisis or emergency. These episodes can and do occur inside as well as outside of psychiatric hospitals and outpatient settings such as clinics and day centers.

Some common causes of crises and/or emergencies in everyday life are:

1. Separation from mother and home in order to start kindergarten or nursery school.

2. Death of a close friend or relative during childhood, or of a loved pet, such as a dog or cat or bird.

3. Leaving home to go to boarding school, prep school, or college.

4. Non-acceptance by peers at school, after moving to a new neighborhood, because of religion, color, or other factors.

5. Serious physical trauma to self or a loved one.

6. Getting engaged or married.

7. Being rejected by a lover.

8. Pregnancy which is unplanned, unwanted, or out-of-wedlock.

9. Being diagnosed as having a more-or-less fatal disease, such as cancer, multiple sclerosis, or leukemia.

10. Loss of a job without believing there is a logical reason for it.

11. Loss of one's independence and acknowledgment of frailty or inadequacy when a son or daughter has to return to the parental home (having been unable to make it in the world-at-large).

12. Being forced to retire from a job without being adequately prepared for retirement.

13. Abandonment by a parent, husband, wife, child, lover, friend, or other significant person(s).

In nearly all of these crises situations, there is the element of "loss"—whether overt or hidden: loss of a loved object; loss of a familiar security agent, device, system, location or person; loss or threatened loss to part of one's body; loss of one's self-esteem, confidence or "face"; loss of one's independence; imminent loss of one's life or someone else's.

Let's look at what happens in the interaction between an individual and his environment which can produce crises and emergencies:

The individual and his environment are in a state of continuous interaction with each other and each has an ongoing regulatory influence on the other—

Individual < ————— > Environment

When the individual feels he has *lost* his capacity to influence, regulate or deal with *the environment,* he begins to feel inadequate to cope with it (life). This environment surrounds him and looms more and more monstrous in his "eyes" and feelings and thoughts.

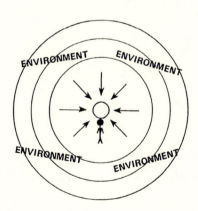

This experience leads to or produces intolerable and seemingly intolerable stress—

and the individual feels increasingly enmeshed, trapped, and engulfed by forces he cannot control or cope with. He may hopelessly give up and become resigned, depressed and mute. Or he may begin to flail wildly and strike out at anything and anyone in his environment as he now moves into a state of *psychiatric emergency.*

The warning signs before the emergency erupts are agitation, aimless pacing with clenched fists, more rapid and heavier breathing, eyes looking wilder and angrier, yelling, throwing things, banging things, becoming demanding and argumentative. (See Chapter 17 on signs of movement towards mental illness.)

The incidence of violent behavior is reduced when the overall attitude towards the patient is respectful, warm, humane and reasonable.

However, in settings where the patient is harassed, pushed, repeatedly demeaned, and treated like an object who is a non-person, the incidence of violent episodes increases as the combination of this environmental irritation added to the personal stress and burdens of the patient leads him to lose control of his angry and violent urges and feelings.

We see then that as a person feels less and less inner self-esteem or significantly respected self while experiencing more and more loss of environmental resources and relationships, his image of himself becomes more and more battered, and he or she feels increasingly isolated, friendless, misunderstood, unaccepted, and vulnerable. At the same moment, the person feels a loss of "face" and loss of "secure self."

He or she now regresses into primitive childlike behavior and responses as he or she moves toward uncontrolled raging—crying—screaming—striking out. He or she becomes for the moment unavailable to ordinary reasoning and logic and feels more impotent, confused, and enraged.

Whether the cry for help is to doctors, clergymen, clinics, emergency rooms, the police, or therapy aides, it is best to approach the patient with two or three team members who have been trained to restrain, control and sedate such violent patients. The approach has to be confident, steady, determined, and calming, with a reassuring voice. Personnel who will be required to work with potentially violent patients should seek (or perhaps demand) training in restraining patients.

While there is still a value in the use of the camisole (straitjacket) for certain patients, it should always be utilized as a *treatment method rather than a punishment method.* Patients should be checked physically quite often when in a camisole, and it should not be used without the prescription of a physician as its use may trigger off profound secondary physical or behavioral reactions, such as a cardiac or cerebro-vascular accident, or elopement from the hospital, or violence towards staff members who are seen as punitive rather than helpful.

We are used to thinking of people developing crises and emergencies as isolated instances. Much of what has been written in this book refers to such persons who create serious episodes of violence towards themselves and others. However, there is a whole group of individuals whom I refer to as "crisis creators" for whom crisis is an expression of their neurotic—not psychotic—way of life. These people get a great deal of excitement, satisfaction, and feelings of aliveness, power, and significance through stirring up a commotion, furor, or crisis in the people or environment around them. They are to be differentiated from and worked with differently than the patients referred to earlier in this chapter.

33

Learning Objectives For Patients

1. To become more comfortable with myself.

2. To learn how to feel I'm worthwhile.

3. To learn to enjoy life more than I do.

4. To learn the language of feelings.

5. To learn to control my impulses.

6. To learn to take more responsibility for my own life.

7. To be less self-centered and more interested in others.

8. To be less dependent.

9. To trust more and be able to be dependent on others.

10. To be able to assert myself more often and more truthfully.

11. To see the glass half full instead of half empty.

12. To see people with new eyes.

13. To give up excessive expectations—to stop expecting what I only have a right to hope for.

14. To learn to live with ambiguity.

15. To be able to live in abeyance.

16. To learn how to work at myself in order to bring about change in myself.

17. To expand my capacity to find or create options.

18. To give up excessive demands by hearing how often

I say "He *should* do that . . ." or "I *should* . . ." or "They *should* . . ."*

19. To give up magical thinking.

20. To stop spiriting away data in order to streamline life.

21. To give up my denial systems.

22. To become aware of and to give up blind spots.

23. To sit quietly with another.

24. To develop more scope in my inner self.

25. To own what's positive in myself and thus to feel at least some of my self-worth.

26. To stop deferring constantly to others and thus become more responsible for me—my own thoughts, my ideas, my happenings.

27. To stop editing and redirecting my conversation on the basis of fear that I'm losing the other person if I don't speak to the topic of his interest.

28. To give up the belief that I am dull, not interesting, and really have nothing valid to say.

29. To be more clear and specific in setting up interpersonal plans and contracts of all types, on a formal and informal basis.

30. To stop deferring and vacillating in making decisions because "something better might come along."

31. To become clearer and to own and act on what I want as I've become clearer about what I don't want.

32. To be more open to receiving the moves of others towards me.

33. To make some decisions for and with action without having to know in advance that they'll be perfect.

34. To give up overconcern with "What they will think?"

35. To learn how to see or create more options in a

---

*Read K. Horney's chapter on "The Tyranny of the Shoulds" in *Neuroses and Human Growth,* Norton & Co., New York, 1950.

given situation and to remain open to them without dismissing them quickly with a "yes, but."

36. To learn the implications of "I'm OK, You're OK" as a way of life.

37. To give up repeating my overly judgmental, demeaning, and tyrannical father and mother in me while I become my own good mother and father to myself.

38. To not let the fear of rejection prevent me from taking risks.

39. To give up my supersensitivity and my feeling of fragility.

40. To be able to express myself truthfully even at times when it carries the risk of not being liked.

41. To give up ruminating.

42. To not let the fear of making a mistake or appearing foolish prevent me from asserting myself or risking taking a particular stand.

43. To give up feeling abused, victimized, or being an injustice and rejection-collector.

44. To see how and when I've been a "help-rejecting complainer" and to work at giving up this way of life.

34

Self-Isolating Mechanisms

Because of the fact that we are all unique and individual persons who, for the most part, live inside our own private, "sealed-in" bodies and minds, we all feel ourselves as separate from others. *This leads to feeling our differentness more often than our similarity to others.* The patients we work with often tend to use their differentness in the service of feeling isolated from others in a self-conscious, uncomfortable, and withdrawn manner.

A person who does not feel sufficient self-esteem, self-worth or self-love cannot feel comfortable when he is with others. He therefore develops techniques which lead him to avoid or withdraw from other people, which further adds to his feeling separated, isolated from, or different from other people whom he endows in his imagination with a constant capacity for ease and joy in their interpersonal involvements.

Patients in outpatient therapy and activity groups, as well as those in hospital inpatient groups, often find some way to define and separate themselves out from others, which is then used to make them feel even worse than they do when they sit alone. *It is a self-defeating, self-negating process which is in the service of self-hate, self-effacement, or escape from the responsibility of risking intimacy, commitment, or involvement with others.*

The self-sorting differentiator is a person dedicated to his own separateness. He can use everything as a basis for isolating himself as "different" or "unacceptable." Some common examples are:

"I'm the only (Jew) (Wasp) (Catholic) in this group."

"I'm the only (Black) (Puerto Rican) (Italian) in this group."

"I'm the only one here with a foreign or different accent (French, Russian, German, deep-south, English, etc.)."

"I'm the only one here who hasn't gone to college."

"I'm the only blue collar worker here."

Understanding this mechanism in yourself may be very helpful in aiding you to spot its occurrence in your patients or clients. It is almost always a self-defeating, self-isolating process.

35

Help-Rejecting Complainers

A help-rejecting complainer° is a patient or non-patient person who is driven compulsively to make verbal and/or non-verbal *demands* on other people to get them *to offer help* in the form of suggestions, guidance, advice *which he then rejects.*

The therapist, mental health aide, peer group members, and others express their attention, time, concern, care, interpretations and advice in response to the felt and stated needs of the help-rejecting complainer—and then, over and over, this help is rejected. The help-rejecting complainer rejects the help with statements like:

"That sounds like a good idea—but I just know it won't work."

"Yes, but do you realize how long that would take?"

"But that's not easy."

"Everybody says that—but they don't know how much I worry that I'll never make it."

No matter how much professional skill, life experience, and practical success are behind the suggestions and advice—the help-rejecting complainer wipes them out and discards them. After becoming increasingly frustrated and irritated, those who have offered help feel "sucked dry" or "taken in." They may then turn on the HRC with anger or rejection because of how the HRC takes their human offerings and twists and wastes them into "nothingness." We then turn away feeling a sense of futility and hopelessness.

It is just at this point that the HRC comes to life in a manner justifying his sense of uniqueness. He says "You see, you don't understand me or my problems which are worse than and different from anyone else's. There's just no hope for me." He now feels proudly justified in maintaining his position.

In attempting to help such a patient, you need to help him examine how much pride he has in maintaining the uniqueness of his "hopeless" condition. He needs to see that it's possible to go beyond being a "glorified nothing" in order to have a sense of significance. He may profit from an examination and realization of the frequency with which he operates with this pattern or system of communicating and relating.

°Also see Berger, M.M. and Rosenbaum, M: "Notes on Help-Rejecting Complainers." *Intl. Jnl. of Group Psychotherapy.* 17:357-370, 1967.

36

On Feeling Abused

There are a number of people who are, in fact, abused by various other people during the course of their life. I refer to children who are exposed to abuse and battering by their parents; to children who are mocked and picked on or teased because of their color, or religion, or a physical condition like a clubfoot, or harelip, or because they wear glasses; to adolescents and adults who are the victims of racism or sexism, etc. These people have a rational basis for feeling abused.

However, there are a large number of people called patients who feel abused much of the time because of their neurotic way of life. We as mental health workers can help them with this self-defeating arrangement by helping them to understand and then, hopefully, to *give up the sequence of events that leads to their chronic abused reaction.*

There is a difference between being abused and feeling abused, although each one can lead to the other!

For a multiplicity of reasons, there occurs in certain people a tendency to develop an image of themselves which tells them that they have a right to make certain claims—often referred to as "neurotic claims"—on others and on life itself.

These claims on others and on life are based on excessive expectations (an excessive expectation exists when I expect what I only have a right to hope for).

Try to list some of the things which you expect from others or from yourself which are not realistic in the sense that you can hope for them or wish for them or make efforts to achieve them, but *which you do not have the right to expect.*

For example, a person who is a compulsive helper may feel self-righteously abused when the help he offers to someone who didn't ask for his help is refused. Or a person who believes that life owes him a living and/or a loving because he has suffered so much may be furious to find he is not loved or rewarded for his suffering and that he is even ignored.

So we see that when a person who makes excessive claims or demands finds his claims or demands ignored or frustrated, he may become angry or furious. However, because he may be enough in touch with reality on some level to question the validity of his claims, he may control his anger and walk around feeling abused and/or depressed. If he is less in touch with reality and does not have adequate self-control, he may strike out verbally or physically with his anger and thus further alienate or separate others from him—which then provides ammunition for the next round or next level of feeling abused. Horney stated: ". . . it is a person's overall defense against coming face to face with himself and his own problems."*

It is crucial that we learn to perceive excessive claims or demands made by others on us or by ourselves on others. We can confront the other person and encourage him to join us in reconsidering the situation in order to avoid an impasse in or break-up of the relationship due to feeling abused.

*Karen Horney: "On Feeling Abused," *Amer. J. of Psychoanalysis*, 11:5-12, 1951. Also see Frederick Weiss: "On feeling Abused and Being Abused," *Amer. J. of Psychoanalysis*, 34:311-314, 1974.

37

Self-Hate

Some examples of self-hate expressed through anxiety as reflected in thoughts are:

"It's too good to happen to me."

"It's not going to last."

"I don't deserve it."

"I can't believe it."

"I'm an outsider, they probably won't accept me."

"He'll probably leave me, like everyone else has whom I cared for."

"What if he finds out my age?"

"I'm so much older than him (or her)."

"I'm so much younger than him (or her)."

"Do I have a right to feel so good?"

"I'd better watch out—something terrible is going to happen because I feel good."

Self-hate is present in all who suffer from neurosis and psychosis. It may express itself in subtle forms, but it is best understood as the opposite of healthy self-love, self-esteem and self-worth.°

Our efforts are aimed at reducing self-hate and increasing self-love as we engage in a remoralization of the patient.°°

°Read about the development and functions of self-hate in the neurotic character structure in Karen Horney's *Neuroses and Human Growth,* Norton & Co., New York 1950.

°°Jerome Frank has written an excellent brief article on remoralization, "Psychotherapy: The Restoration of Morale," *American J. of Psychiatry,* Vol. 131, No. 3, p. 271-274, March, 1974.

Direct and indirect forms of self-hate° include but are not limited to:

Self-belittling: "It was nothing. I shouldn't get credit for that. It was just luck."

Self-derision: "I'm just stupid. I always do crazy things like that."

Self-effacement: "You shouldn't have bothered."

Self-neglect: "I'm too busy to go shopping for myself."

Self-vindictive criticism: "I'm such a fool I don't deserve anything better than that. Sometimes I even question if I deserve to live."

Self-excoriation: Picking at one's face or scalp until it is raw, bleeding and painful.

Self-abuse: Punching a wall or a hole through a glass window to express anger or frustration.

Self-flagellation: Head-banging.

Self-deprivation: Not fulfilling one's wants or needs because of a feeling of unworthiness.

Self-ridiculing: Exposing one's weaknesses or failures to others to provoke laughter at the expense of self.

Suicide attempts—whether they be typical attempts by wrist-cutting or swallowing large numbers of pills, or slow suicide attempts such as overuse of alcohol, tobacco, drugs, excess food intake, or neglect of one's body.

°See *Compassion and Self-Hate* by Theodore Rubin, M.D., David McKay, New York, 1975, for a full delineation of the subtleties of self-hate.

38

The Silent Patient

Patients are silent for many reasons. Among the most common causes is their fear that what they might say will come out in a fashion that will lead to disapproval and/or rejection.

"It will sound stupid."
"It will not be perfect."
"It will not be nice."
"It will be inappropriate."
"They will not like me for saying it."
"People will find out what I'm really like and then they will not like me."
"I am basically shy for fear I may be laughed at, told I'm wrong, ridiculed, mocked, made to feel like a nothing."
"I don't know what is the right thing to say; so I think it's better to keep my mouth shut."
"I am shy in order to avoid contact with people, because once we start talking it could lead to a sexual involvement and I'm scared of that."
"I'm afraid to initiate something for fear of being considered pushy."
"I don't want people to think I have loose morals."

In approaching patients who are silent it may be helpful to ask:

"What blocks you from speaking?"

"What are you afraid will happen if you talk about
what is going on in you?"

"What's the worst calamity that can happen if you
speak up?"

"Is it hard for you to believe I could really be interested in you?"

"You seem to be suffering. Perhaps I could be of
help to you if you'd let me know what's going on
in you."

39 Self-Assertion Versus Neurotic Aggressivity

Is there a difference between healthy self-assertiveness and neurotic aggressiveness? Yes, there surely is.

Healthy self-assertion means the act of asserting oneself or one's rights *without* any compulsive, blind, uncaring, selfish, self-centered disregard for the rights of others! It includes the relatively free expression at the appropriate time and in the appropriate setting or context of one's wishes. (*"If no one is sitting on that seat, I'd appreciate your moving your coat so I could sit there. Thanks for your cooperation."*) Other expressions include:

> one's opinions (*"It's my opinion that he didn't have the right to jeopardize all of us without consulting with us first."*)
>
> warranted criticisms (*"I thought it was done in a very unfeeling and insensitive manner."*)
>
> one's feelings (*"I get angry when people attempt to embarrass me in a public situation."*)
>
> one's rights (*"I have the right to be waited on first. I was in line ten minutes before them."*)

Healthy self-assertion includes doing something in one's own interest, such as competing for a scholarship, or giving orders to people when you have the right to, and selecting the people you want to associate with. It therefore means *you have to learn the art of giving and receiving rejection as well as compliments and affection.*

Healthy self assertion includes having the ability, as well as the right, to say NO even though other people attempt to guilt-provoke you by saying or acting as if their feelings are hurt. It means being able to say NO to an invitation you don't want to accept.

Contrary to healthy self-assertion, neurotic aggressivity implies the process of acting against someone else by encroaching on his rights, or person, or spatial-geographical territory. It may mean disregarding, pushing, exploiting, attacking, or disparaging the other person.

Such aggressive behavior may be manifested by a tendency to be domineering, over-exacting, cheating, manipulating, humiliating, or putting down the other person by continuous or excessive fault-finding. This may give the temporarily gratifying feelings of a vindictive triumph.

Whereas healthy self-assertiveness is based on wholehearted, free, sincere, and reliable inner convictions and feelings for others as well as self, neurotic aggressiveness is compulsive, indiscriminate, and insatiable.

The aggressive person may be that way in order to compensate for basic feelings of anxiety and timidity and smallness and is expressing his significance by moving against others.°

A more elusive but common form of neurotic aggressivity is shown by persons described as having "a passive-aggressive personality." Their antagonistic, oppositional, provocative behavior is manifested in such acts as "accidentally" burning holes in your rugs or furniture with their hot cigarette ashes, giving people the "silent treatment" instead of engaging in open dialogue to clear up interpersonal confusion and difficulties, or doing jobs they are responsible for in a sloppy, incomplete manner which carries the message "fuck you" and leaves a situation requiring others to finish or redo what they've started. Oppositional persons tend to be argumentative and when confronted often respond with, "What's the matter? Don't I have the right to ask why?"

Neurotic aggressive persons have often given up their interest in being loved and accepted for goals which are more significant to them, namely, power, attention, getting even with vindictive triumphs, and possibly enjoying a strange sense of glory in being the most significantly disliked person. They may have a feeling of neurotic pride in behaviors which spirit them away from feelings of being "insignificant" or "nothing."

°See Karen Horney's book *Neuroses and Human Growth*, W. W. Norton & Co., New York, 1950, for a thorough description and explanation of "moving towards," "moving against," and "moving away from" others.

40 Competency In the Art Of Daily Living

Following are some of the basic qualities and skills necessary to get along with others in day-to-day life:

—*Effective Communication Skills:*
  Listening—Comprehending.
  Interrupting—Speaking Convincingly.
  Reading Non-Verbal Gestures and Body Language.
  Speaking to the Point—Asking.
—*Ability to Abstract and Analyze.*
—*Ability to Connect.*
—*Conflict and Problem Solving Skills.*
—*Ability to Make Independent Value Judgments.*
—*Facility in Social Interaction:*
  A respect for others' rights, differences, space.
  A constructive, open, non-oppositional attitude.
—*Understanding the Relationship Between Oneself, Other People and the Environment.*
—*Awareness of the Personal World in Which We Live and the World-At-Large Which Extends Beyond Our Self.*
—*An Awareness of How We Are Perceived By Others.*
—*An Awareness and Response to the Arts, Humanities and Political Systems.*
—*Enough Humility to Maintain a Sense of Humor.*
—*That Degree and Quality of Common Sense which Are Based on a Sense of Appropriateness and Timing.*

41

Sleep

Sleep is important to maintain a "healthy" equilibrium and is often disturbed in nervous and emotionally disturbed patients.

Insomnia or *having trouble sleeping* occurs in about 85% of depressed patients.

Sleep disturbances fall into a number of different patterns. The clearer you are about the details, the more accurate will be your method of dealing with the sleep problems.

Common patterns are:

1. The person who has increased sleep. It serves as a method of avoidance and withdrawal.

2. Some persons cannot fall asleep because of tension, anxiety, or a fear of losing control.

3. A number of people wake in the middle of the night—usually because of disturbing dreams.

4. Another group awaken very early in the morning and then cannot fall asleep again. If they take medication at this hour, which does put them to sleep, they may awaken groggy, dizzy, tired, as if with a hangover, or may get up to look for work and thus trigger off a secondary series of problems.

5. People who say they "didn't sleep a wink all night"—due to the fact that their sleep was light and restless—although they actually did sleep to some extent.

All patients who complain about sleep should be listened to carefully and taken seriously. In addition to psychotherapy, medication, or other approaches to the problem of falling asleep, I have found it is often of value to suggest that they think of something pleasant, such as a happy summer vacation in childhood, thus moving their thought content from a present anxiety situation to a more distant anxiety-free time and location. They may have to make a repeated effort to change their thought content from that which is troublesome to that which is more pleasant.

In more recent times, the growing interest in meditation and emptying one's mind of anxiety-connected thoughts has led to an increasing use of an exercise in which you close your eyes, breathe in and out slowly and deeply, saying nothing while you inhale but saying "mmmmmmmmm . . ." or "ommmmmmmm . . ." quietly as you exhale and, at the same time, attempt to move your mental pictures towards empty space.

Most of the tranquilizing medications can be effective if given in a large dose at bedtime, as they not only last through a 24-hour period but also help to promote a deeper and longer lasting sleep. This allows the patient to be more alert and active during the daytime.

An increasingly popular but surprisingly difficult method to reduce tension and promote relaxation and sleep is to suggest that the patient try to think of 5 or 10 nice things about himself and repeat the list a number of times. This can be very effective. Try it yourself.

42

Dreams

In the middle ages a rabbi said that "to have a dream and not examine the possible meaning is like receiving a letter and not opening it!"

We are the architects of our own dreams! Our dreams more truthfully represent what is going on in our deepest unconscious inner self than any other communication to ourselves and others. As children so often experience, our dreams may reflect simple wish-fulfillment in an open or disguised form, or they may represent more complicated inner conflicts, feelings, and anxieties about problems in our present life which we are "allergic" to because of our past experiences. Our past is always existent in our present moment!

It is important to respect dreams and to encourage the dreamer to remember his dreams as important data to be presented for "working-through" to his therapist. The dreamer should realize, too, that he is the recipient of a gift—from his own unconscious functioning—which may allow him to become more aware of what deep down in his guts he really feels, wishes, wants, or values, or about which he is anxious and in conflict. This valuable information is available to each of us *"at no extra charge."*

In our society we were all raised in childhood with almost all of our behavior and functioning judged as either "good or bad," "right or wrong," "perfect or imperfect," "acceptable or unacceptable." These values served to constrict our freedom to function as living, changing human beings whose basic nature is to grow and be constructive for ourselves and others if given a chance to do so.

The psychotherapeutic process which includes the examination of dreams starts with encouraging patients to accept the contents of dreams without prejudging them as "good or bad," "right or wrong," "acceptable or unacceptable." Then we can look at them as our living process and examine them in terms of: "What is going on?" "Where?" "When?" "With whom?" "Preceded by what?" "Followed by what?" "How do I feel about this?" "Is this familiar to me and if so from what situation? With whom? When? Where?" Thus I, the dreamer, can begin to make sense out of what would otherwise not be understandable. The dreamer can thus learn more about the process of communicating with himself in symbolic, disguised messages which carry a deeper hidden or latent content and which bring him more knowledge about himself. As the dreamer gets more in touch with himself, he may learn to respect the inner wisdom of his body and mind and to be more open to what goes on outside of his conscious awareness in the areas of his being which serve as warehouse for all earlier experiences and memories.

As the dreamer is educated to be responsible for what goes on inside himself, he finds it more and more difficult to deny that he is the architect of his own dreams. As this occurs, he is able to see and accept more of the responsibility for his own life and for what happens to him in his daily living as well. He is able to be increasingly motivated, to examine his own role in arranging for what happens to him in his life, and to reduce the tendency to attribute responsibility to others for what happens to him.

We can see this in the following dream:

A 46-year-old, American-born, married accountant with two children reports, "I dreamed I was shitting on myself—I was naked and I couldn't stop it—vaguely afterwards I was aware of making efforts to clean up the mess I'd made." In reflecting upon the possible implications of this dream, we agreed that it was not necessarily a "bad," "crazy," or "ridiculous" dream because dreams use (overt) symbols and signs to carry more complicated (latent) hidden, deeper messages. In this dream he was stating his increasing aware-

ness that he was somehow getting the "short end of the stick" in his life—that is, winding up feeling "shit upon"—not getting what pleasure and satisfaction he really deserves in view of how hard he works and how much he does for others, especially his wife and his children. In reviewing the dream, he began to realize how much he "shits" upon himself—upon his own real feelings, wishes, and wants—in his everyday life, at work, and with his family. This seemingly "bad" dream served to awaken in him his awareness of his own responsibility for what was happening in his life and the need for him to change in his reactions with others if he wanted his life with others to be different.

Dreams often reflect where the dreamer has been in his earlier life experiences, where he is now, and, sometimes, imply or offer options for where he could be in future situations if he were willing to commit himself to the effort and dedication required to bring about change.

There are no such things as "bad" dreams. There are dreams which are disturbing, anxiety-provoking, conflict-ridden, nightmarish, and which lead us to awaken from sleep. But it is not logical that we consider them bad because we may need to go through a shocking nightmare to finally awaken to and attempt to resolve deep inner conflicts. And with such coming to grips with inner conflicts, we may be able to risk moving our own growing edge forward.

43 There Are Many Approaches To Patients

There are as many ways to approach and greet patients as there are to approach anyone you meet.

"I am here."
"Where are you?"

1. Greetings can be:
   a) Verbal:
      (1) personal ("Hi, Jerry," or "Good morning, Mr. Thomas.")
      (2) impersonal ("Hi")
   b) Nonverbal:
      (1) Ignoring is a form of greeting —by nonacknowledgment.
      (2) Inviting—coming to a stop in front of the patient as a prelude to an encounter or conversation.
      (3) Casual—while passing by.

2. Questioning: "How are you?" "How's your world today?"

3. Clarification of what a patient is saying or doing—in a direct manner or a non-directive manner. For example, "You seem to be expressing anger with your fists. Would you like to talk about it?"

4. Acceptance of a patient's right to say or feel things that are irrational, bizarre, or inappropriate while making clear that you do not agree or believe that the thoughts, feelings, or actions are based on reality. For example, "Harry, I hear what you're saying." (We've learned that there is meaning in seemingly crazy expressions or utterances.)

5. A direct confrontation with your response, i.e., your thought and/or feeling response to the patient/client's statement or behavior. For example, "I don't feel that this would be appropriate right now."

6. Facilitating expression of thoughts and/or feelings. For example, "Do you think you might be trying to say: 'I'd rather my mother didn't visit me again.'?"

7. Discouraging acting-out behaviors or inappropriate behaviors while encouraging patient/client to talk about "what is going on in him" now.

8. Acknowledging the patient/client and engaging him in dialogue with "I'd like to hear your opinion about this . . ."
   or "What's going on in you right now? Harry . . ."
   or "How do you feel about this?"
   or "Is this OK with you?"

or "Do you mind if I join you?"

or "Do you agree that Harry has a good idea there?"

or "Do you think Harry ought to stop and think about it before he does that?"

9. Communicating acceptance (verbally and nonverbally). Don't make remarks which are separating and make people feel their differentness, such as, "I wonder what *you people* think about what's going on here today?"

10. Explaining that nodding my head means *"I hear you"* and not that "I approve or agree with you."

11. Praise or reward the patient/client with a comment on evidence of personal or interpersonal competency in handling a situation with another patient, staff member, or a relative, or in a telephone call. (Praise or positive regard can be expressed with a congratulatory handshake, with a smile of approval accompanied by a positive nod of the head, or by some other expression of approval, admiration, or affirmation. This needs to be done often and is the path towards building or rebuilding self-esteem and self-confidence.)

12. Reinforcement techniques—suggesting a patient say or do something again, with more enthusiasm, or interest, or physical expression.

13. Repetition of what the patient/client says or repetition of what you have just said—and following it with the question, "Do you understand what I've just said?" or "Would you like me to repeat it?" This is particularly important in our relationship with patients receiving medication.

14. Asking patient/client if he can think of any other solutions, options, alternatives, or choices to solve his problems. And then offering him other solutions, options, alternatives, or choices to think about. If in a group setting, ask other group members if they can offer the patient any other options or possible solutions.

15. Offering support and/or encouragement and/or hope.

16. Offering empathy—sympathy—compassion.

17. Suggesting role-playing or behavior rehearsal scenes.

18. Suggesting sensitivity awareness, risk-taking, or trust exercises.

44 Do's and Don'ts To Improve Self-Esteem

Encourage patients by acknowledging their efforts towards change and growth! Whenever possible, offer approval, praise, and attention to their creativity or living up to responsibility for self and others. This will improve their self-image and self-esteem, and bolster their hopefulness and their relationship with you. Avoid putdowns!

DO'S	DON'TS
"I like the way you said that."	*No comment* is made in answer to the patient's statement.
"You look a lot better this morning than when you arrived two weeks ago."	"Oh! You've changed your hair. *Why did you* do it this way?"
"I liked the way you asked for that."	"*Why* do you want it?"
"I liked the way you spoke to your mother then."	"So you spoke to your mother."
"I appreciate your helping me with this."	"OK. Thanks."
"You look so much better when you comb your hair."	"Oh! *So you've finally* put yourself together like a lady!"
"I know you're improving because you no longer go back to bed after breakfast."	"So, Jack, what are you going to do today after breakfast?" (*sarcastically*)
"I know you're improving because you take more initiative in bringing problems up for discussion."	"You're really getting quite rambunctious at community meetings now, *aren't you?*"

DO'S	*DON'TS*
"I know you're improving because your attitude isn't so antagonistic when you differ with somebody else."	"Do you *always* have to disagree?"
"You're right. He is difficult. I usually move away from people when they act like that."	"You've *got to* learn to get along with everybody."
"I hope you'll tell your doctor about that because he may be better able to help you understand it."	"Why bother me with that? Save it for your doctor."

45

Groups For Therapy and Growth

Group psychotherapy refers to all those regularly scheduled and voluntarily attended or accepted meetings of acknowledged patients with an acknowledged, trained psychotherapist for the purpose of expressing, eliciting, accepting, and working through one's biosocial psychopathological functioning and developing one's healthier potentials. During group therapy, the patient will communicate, relate and work with others in a corrective, interactional, re-educative, emotional, and attitudinal experience focusing on individual and group dynamics in a spirit of trust, mutuality and confidentiality.

Understanding, experiencing, and motivation are the necessary requirements for real and lasting change which can occur in an atmosphere where peer support provides the matrix for a feeling of acceptance and belonging.

The goal of group psychotherapy is the elicitation, recognition, acceptance, understanding, and resolution or working through of intrapsychic and interpersonal psychopathology.[*]

In group psychotherapy, the experiential is valued more highly than the intellectual in coming to grips with one's conflicts and hangups. The prerequisite for change is based more on experiencing through interacting than on intellectual, deductive processes which may lead to intellectual insight but not to basic change. Change through emotional and experiential risk-taking is the common course in group psychotherapy. This is particularly true when intellectual understanding accompanies the experiential phenomena which erupt spontaneously and creatively, as well as through appropriate therapeutic interventions. However, at times basic personality change can occur in group psychotherapy without understanding.

A therapy group:
—is permissive;
—offers peer or sibling support and not just sibling rivalry;
—offers an opportunity to give up

---

[*]For an overview of the historical development of group therapeutic approaches ranging from inspirational to didactic to activity to psychoanalytic work in groups, and for a comprehensive sampling of the many varied group approaches for therapy and growth, the reader is referred to *Group Psychotherapy and Group Function* by M. Rosenbaum and M. Berger, 2nd Edition, Basic Books, New York, 1975.

emotional illiteracy;

—is stimulating in the ways that it confronts:

    —by asking questions;

    —by offering advice;

    —by offering new options and possible solutions;

—offers an opportunity to reenact long-term, self-defeating patterns learned in one's early family and school life.

—makes possible a corrective emotional experience allowing for new patterns to be tested out with realistic feedback or validation from other group members.

A therapy group offers an opportunity:

—to express anger without retribution so that the true source of this anger can be examined and understood;

—to learn social skills and the art of daily living;

—to learn how to work constructively with others on immediate and long range goals;

—to give to others as well as receive;

—to learn the art of receiving acceptance and approval, as well as the art of being rejecting without destroying other people;

—to change through experiencing and not solely through gaining insights or understanding.

46 Why Is There So Much Emphasis On Groups?

Many patients participate in more than one group concurrently. They may be in a psychotherapy group, a morning and/or afternoon therapeutic community group meeting, a daily activities group, a family group, a special task-oriented work or learning group, a rehabilitation group using art, poetry or music, and a recreational group.

There are many values to such participation in multiple groups. The numerous contacts, interactions, stimulations, communications and crosscultural experiences offer such advantages as:

1. opportunities for a sense of *belonging*. It is difficult to maintain one's sense of isolation, pathological uniqueness, and unworthiness when there is acceptance by so many people in different groups.

2. opportunities to learn about the many varieties of human functioning, values, and experience which until now they had not known. Thus, impoverishment is decreased as one evaluates the similarities and differences between oneself and those from other socio-economic-ethnic backgrounds.

3. fostering a sense of universality as we learn of our sameness with other people.

4. many more opportunities to find, communicate with, and relate to a significant other person.

5. being compelled to accept "how much 'I' as a patient tend to project or externalize what is really going on in me onto others." With a sense of warmth, humor, and lightness, group members can help a paranoid person see the irrationality and grandiosity of his persecutory ideas and feelings.

6. more opportunities to be confronted with rationalizations, evasions, distortions, and blind spots. One patient said, "You can easily believe one group is against you, but it is much, much harder to believe two or three separate groups are against you."

7. more freedom to experiment with new ways of behaving—new attempts to trust others, to risk asking for something for oneself, to assert oneself or to reach out toward another person with affection or positive regard.

8. experiences in groups which encourage and foster each member's active involvement and responsibility. The achievement of the group's objectives increases feelings of equality and mutuality, while nurturing each person's capacity for risk-taking and cooperating with others. Satisfaction is experienced in the joy of working with others, and individuals can become less obsessed with winning and with "proving" how great one is.

9. opportunities to speak and behave in order to express oneself rather than to impress others!

47　The Therapeutic Alliance

We have gradually understood that emotionally and mentally disturbed patients and clients do not become well for a sustained period of time simply by our *doing something to them or for them,* as in the usual medical model where a patient comes for a diagnosis and expects to receive a pill or injection or advice which will "cure" him.

While there is a value in being offered a pill or injection or advice, we find that the treatment is most likely to be of help when the patient is actually, voluntarily and wholeheartedly engaged in and participating in the treatment plan designed for him. Engaging him more actively as a participant in planning and carrying out his own journey towards "health" is expedited when one or more members of the helping team can forge a *therapeutic alliance* with the patient or client.

The therapeutic alliance is based on the patient's feeling that he is respected as a person by the helping person(s) and that he can trust such person(s). This can occur if he has been helped to believe in and experience the helper's sincere capacity for and expression of an empathetic attitude towards him and his "situation." He can now accept that he is seen as an individual and not as a "case" or "number" or "object."

When he believes he is accepted rather than condemned or blamed for feeling, thinking, or being as he is, he can willingly form an alliance with the helper(s) to understand the basis for his maladaptive way of life. He can risk trying new ways of seeing, understanding, and behaving when alone and with others. He needs your continuing encouragement and support to risk change.

He can risk changing when he finds that the atmosphere and attitudes of others towards him are different from what he has previously found in his family or in society-at-large.

As he engages in a "therapeutic alliance," the patient-person feels better about himself and is thus motivated even more to engage himself in efforts which give him a greater sense of adequacy, security, significance, and self-esteem. (See page 79 on *Competency In the Art of Daily Living.)*

A therapeutic alliance, then, is a gradually developing, mutually respected, spoken and unspoken contract between a helping person and a patient or client. Its purpose and method are to voluntarily trust each other's sincerity in examining, communicating, understanding, and changing the daily functioning of the patient-person so that he is capable of taking charge of his own life in a goal-directed fashion. This includes a realistic appraisal of and capacity to understand and respect the rights and wishes of others, while struggling to fulfill his own potential.

The nuances of the human condition and of interpersonal relationships are so numerous and so subtle that, in order to become competent or skilled in functioning with people-in-the-world-at-large, the patient can benefit from having a different therapeutic alliance with each member of the psychiatric team. While one helps him to understand the value of healthy conformity or compliance with authority figures, another staff member may be helping the patient understand the impact of his nonverbal attitudes and behaviors on others. (See page 103 on Nonverbal Communications.) Each staff member of a treatment center can have a different constructive value for each patient.

48

Goal Planning

Goal planning,[*] or learning by objectives, is based on the idea that if you don't know where you want to go, all roads will get you there, but you won't know you're there when you arrive! And if you do know what you want, what your objectives are—then you and your patient can work together to achieve those goals! It is important that the patient clearly understand and accept the goals.

The five main steps involved in goal planning are:

1. *Involve the patient.* Discuss possible goals with him and direct your energies towards goals which the patient accepts as being meaningful for him or her.

2. *Set reasonable goals.* Don't set goals which are beyond the patient's *present* level of functioning in view of how he is right now—his life experiences and his resources. You can set additional or different goals at a later time.

3. *Describe and explain the implications of the patient's behavior when the goal is reached.* The patient needs to be able to read the objective which may be written up like a contract and must agree with you as to what it means and that he is motivated to work cooperatively with you to achieve it.

4. *Set a date of completion (or "Deadline").* Pick a date which is feasible—which allows for this patient to complete the established goal. While the date can be moved back, if necessary, there is a structural value in having an estimated date of completion to work toward.

5. *Spell out the method of working procedure in detail.* Clarify just who will do what, in which order and be as clear and specific as possible so that a third person could read it and understand clearly the intent and plan.

AND BE SURE TO PRAISE THE PATIENT FOR HIS EFFORTS!

[*]This material is derived from *Goal Planning in Mental Health Rehabilitation* by Peter S. Houts and Robert A. Scott, 47-page illustrated booklet published in 1972. Write to authors at Department of Behavioral Science, Pennsylvania State University, College of Medicine, Milton S. Hershey Medical Center, Hershey, Pennsylvania.

49

Communications

Communications occur through multiple, different, mutually modifying channels and at multiple, different levels simultaneously. When there is a general sense of harmony, consistency, and uniformity of the messages being conveyed at any one moment through the multiple available levels for communication, we have a sense of knowing what the other person is saying and where we are with him or her. However, when the messages coming to us from another person at any one moment through different channels and at different levels are different, contradictory, ambivalent, or unclear we find ourselves confused, perplexed, unsure, and increasingly anxious.

When a person in a two-person communication system is the recipient of frequent mutually-contradictory messages which leave him with confusion and a feeling of being "on the ropes" as if punchy, we say he is the recipient of a "double-binding" communication. The receiver feels, "I can never be right" or "I can't win."

A popular joke that in an overly simplistic manner makes the double-bind[*] clear tells of a mother who visits her son at boarding school and brings him two ties for his birthday—a red one and a blue one. The following week he comes home to have dinner with his parents and his mother notices he's wearing the blue tie as he walks in the door. She greets him with, "I see you're wearing the blue tie I gave you. What's the matter? You didn't like the red one?"

In working with patients, it is important that we be aware of all channels of communication and not use any of them to transmit confusing, contradictory or negative messages. What are some of these channels for communications?

1. There are messages we *hear* through our ears. The meanings and implications, along with the code as to how to interpret the messages, is conveyed by tone, pitch, rhythm, inflection, speed, intensity, repetition, pauses and accent, as well as by the words themselves.

[*]G. Bateson, D.D. Jackson, J. Haley, J. Weakland, "Toward A Theory of Schizophrenia," *Behavior Science* 1:251-264, 1956. This basic article first presented the revolutionary concept of the "double-bind." That article provided much of the basis for our present day understanding that "the most important aspect of social behavior is its communicative effect and . . . communication is the major factor in the ordering of behavior socially," as stated by John Weakland in "The Double-Bind Theory by Self-Reflexive Hindsight," *Family Process* 13:269-277, 1974.

2. There are messages we *see* through direct human behaviors which declare truthfully *what* is going on, but not necessarily *why* it is going on. There are messages which are signs and messages which are symbols.

3. Our *smelling* sensors, or olfactory apparatus, are located in our nose and messages are communicated to our brain after we smell what is going on in our environment. Dogs and other forms of life depend more on smelling for communication and survival than man does. Smelling is a primitive function which serves not only to warn us of certain potential dangers (such as escaping "gas" or the smell of fish or meat going "bad"), but also to inform us of seductive body odors and perfumes intended to enhance sexual attraction. A common phrase to communicate the need for alertness is, "I smell something rotten here."

4. Our *tasting* apparatus is located in our mouths and primarily mediated through our taste-buds on our tongue. Tasting is a basic sensory function which communicates many things to us. As individuals, we more-or-less like or don't like the taste of our sexual partners or relatives. We like the taste of the food we are served or we don't, and then may decide not to eat it because it may be contaminated. Our patients often refer to food not tasting right or being poisoned to express their suspiciousness, their anxiety and their paranoid position. A common phrase of disapproval is, "This just doesn't suit my taste!"

5. *Tactile* communications carry data coming from our position in space and the physical environment we are in contact with. The fluid in our semicircular canals in our inner-ear moves when we bend or tilt or are in danger of falling and this data informs us, so we become alerted and attempt to correct our body position to one which is safer and more comfortable. Another one of our tactile or touching senses functions through nerve endings in our skin tissues, especially in our feet. Messages are communicated to our brain as to how we are standing and what we are standing on—that is, are we standing on solid ground? Or perhaps on shifting sands which means we are in a more precarious position. These messages which are communicated to our brain provide data for executive decisions as to the nature and degree of danger (based on this data plus data from our other senses) and what to do about it.

Touching one another is a major and extremely meaningful aspect of interpersonal relationships. We may enjoy or recoil from the touch of another person depending on who the person is, the softness or roughness of the touch, the time, location, part of our body which is being touched, the context of the touching situation, and whether there is a covert message in the touch or just a straight message.

In our work, the appropriateness of touching another person physically is open to question and examination. It is important to have a rationale to account for our interventions and to document whether results show our move to be protherapeutic or antitherapeutic.

In our society many people are hungry to be hugged or touched, but *we have to be careful not to exploit our patients' need because of our personal need.*

Communicating as part of a two-or-more-person-interaction requires *Speaking, Listening, Understanding, Interrupting* and *Interacting.*

50

Communication— Speaking

Patients have difficulty in communicating adequately through speaking for some of the following reasons:

1. They don't say what they mean.

2. They hedge or over-qualify their remarks.

3. They speak around the edges of their subject while getting furious at others who don't clearly and completely understand what they mean. There is a magical expectation here that others *should* understand them.

4. They whine in an obnoxious, insidious, childlike way which "turns off" listeners.

5. They start a topic, retreat, go over the same things again and again, making a sort of "overkill."

6. They speak in a disjointed, scattered fashion so the listener loses the main point (if there is one).

7. They may so embellish their stories that they always come out as a helpless victim of others or of circumstances; after others become familiar with this repetitive pattern, they lose interest.

8. They dilute a statement while they are making it.

9. They speak without appropriate affect or nonverbal gestures to emphasize and support their content.

10. They may make a strong and clear verbal statement but contradict it simultaneously with a nonverbal statement, such as a childlike smile or "shit-eating grin."

11. They communicate an attitude towards themselves which says to others, "Don't really listen to me as I'm not really significant enough to be heard." They communicate a massive degree of self-effacement indicating that "I am a nobody."

12. They interrupt their remarks with the phrase "you know" too often.

13. Some speak too quietly and monotonously.

14. Some are just plain boring.

15. They may be in awe of or frightened by another person because they are "allergic" or overly sensitive to whatever or whoever that other person is for them. For example, the other per-

son may be an authority figure who reminds the patient of one or both of his critical, tyrannical, demeaning parents, or of his teachers with whom he or she could never feel "right" or accepted.

16. They speak to *impress* rather than to *express*.

17. They talk to *perform* and *prove* rather than to be real and to provide understanding of their feelings, thoughts, or behavior.

18. They talk as if they are "walking on eggshells" for such reasons as fear of being "wrong," "caught," "imperfect," or otherwise not coming through as they think they should.

19. They flood the interactional interchange with verbal garbage which is essentially "much-ado-about-nothing." This verbal garbage must be differentiated from the communications of a psychotic patient whose dissociated and fragmented thoughts lead him to pour out a "word-salad," or seemingly incoherent phrases which contain major references to what is really troubling him.

20. They use conversation to "assault" or "put down" other persons in an attempt to pierce through their armor which they then struggle even harder to maintain.

21. They are insensitive to the perplexity or lack of understanding of others, and don't listen or know how to interrupt.

22. They employ words or phrases which are beyond the grasp of others.

23. They are busy explaining and over-explaining and justifying when no explanation or justification is necessary.

24. They are "compulsive-talkers" and can only be adapted to by the other persons tuning them out.

25. They preface their comments with the phrase, "To tell you the truth. . . ." The listener may give up full attention to listening while he wonders how much of what the speaker says is really the truth.

26. They find it difficult to open up about intimate feelings in a group. Opening up to more than one person seems to do away with the sense of intimacy, because for such persons intimacy and secrecy go together.

27. They find it difficult or impossible to express any strong emotion at the moment it is happening because it is experienced as going out of control.

51

Communication— Listening

Problems in listening which lend confusion to the communication process are:

1. Having a preconceived closed position so that one's attitude says, "Please don't confuse me with new data. I've already made up my mind. I'm not really listening."

2. A lack of wholehearted interest in any of the communicators or their messages.

3. Preoccupation with other (outside this communicational situation) problems which are more pressing than what is being spoken of.

4. Listening with an offensive-defensive oppositional attitude as if one has a preprogrammed position against the issue and, therefore, looks for evidence of being ignored, demeaned, or otherwise put down.

5. When one isn't listening to the nonverbal messages along with the words and tone in the context of the situation during the discussion.

6. Screening out or distorting (as with a "slip-of-the-ear") certain words, phrases, tones, or content, leading to inadequate perception of meaning.

7. Perceptual distortions so that a word is heard wrongly (sort of a slip-of-the-hearing) and the distortion is then reacted to with anger or, inappropriately, as if it (the distortion) were really what was said.

8. Not hearing the real message of the other person because he or she has arrogantly been brushed off or dismissed by the listener as being insignificant and, therefore, not capable of saying anything significant.

9. When there exists an increasing hearing deficit which is unrecognized and not dealt with. Such a hearing loss may be due to wax in the ears, increasing deafness in the aging years, or a brain tumor.

10. "Tuning out" because the messages are too painful to hear even though they may be true.

11. Not listening with one's "third ear"— not listening to what our body is telling us as we listen with our ears.

12. Hearing the other person as "patronizing" and not confronting him or her with your feeling-reaction.

13. Misunderstandings due to outside noises or other distracting events.

52

Communication— Understanding

Problems in understanding occur because:

1. The listener is not listening wholeheartedly, being preoccupied with something more important to him.

2. The data presented are too complicated in the form they are presented; they are too technical, too abstract, or too unrelated to the other person and his life experience.

3. The communications are not comprehensible to the listener because there is a "block"—an emotional block to the person speaking or to the content of what is being said.

4. The data are either above or below the listener's usual intellectual level of functioning.

Some examples of what goes on between people to prevent real understanding are quoted here verbatim from a psychotherapy group:

"You wrap your communications in such a package that it is hard to unwrap them and be open to receiving what you say is your concern . . ."

"You obfuscate matters . . ."

"You speak as if yours is the last word —received from the Lord at the top of the mountain."

"You somehow move me away from you as you talk."

"As you talk, you communicate that you want to be served on a silver platter and that you don't want to put both your hands into the mixing bowl, so I tune you out."

"You compliment and put me down at the same time and so I can't understand what you're really saying to me."

"I discount a lot of what you say because you often seem to say irrelevant things or somehow knock them out of balance."

"You speak in such a way that it seems to be more important how you say things than that I really hear you and understand you. It's like you're speaking for yourself rather than for me to hear you. It's as if you're busy speaking to put your 'two cents' into the conversation rather than to reach across to the rest of us."

"Somehow you stop the flow of conversation. You close things so there's no bridge from your thoughts to mine." (This lack of flow, of questioning, seems to indicate a lack of desire to hear more from or understand the reactions, feelings, or thoughts of others.)

53

Communication— Interrupting

Problems in interrupting occur:

1. When a person may be afraid to interrupt because he will be considered "rude," "impolite," "not nice," "not respectful." The fear of interrupting usually is based upon having been tyrannized during childhood by parents or teachers who said, "Children are to speak only when told to or asked questions." One woman remembers that as a child she was told over and over again that "Children and fish are not allowed to talk at the table."

2. Out of fear that "You'll think I am inappropriate, wrong, or the dumb shit I think I am or I think you think I am."

3. Out of a feeling that "What I have to say is not really important." This comes out of being beaten down in childhood and feeling little or no self-esteem unless one makes a brilliant contribution. A patient says, "I don't feel I have the kind of insight and understanding the rest of you do, so it's better to keep my mouth shut."

4. Out of a feeling that "If I interrupt and talk about what's on my mind—which is really what's important—you'll be angry and won't like me, or at the least won't be able to understand me."

5. Because of an inner self-concept that says, "I never see things as other people do" which the person was told over and over again in childhood, with the mocking phrase: "Ha, ha! Everyone's out of step but you."

6. When the motivation of the interrupter is primarily to gain attention rather than to seek clarification or add something pertinent to the dialogue. This is a common pattern in children not receiving "adequate" attention in their lives.

7. When one person involved in the dialogue is under great pressure to speak because of the fear that he will lose the thought in his mind if he doesn't say it immediately. This may occur if that person believes his thought is a very important thought because it is *his* thought! And he wants to register it before someone else does to get credit for his brilliance or to get it out before the theme of the conversation changes.

54

Communication— Interacting

Problems in interacting occur:

1. When one person's communications are self-contained, closing-type statements, he or she does not offer a bridge to the other person to keep an open system functioning. The message sent is, "I don't need anything from you. I don't need to hear you say anything about the details of your life or experiences or reactions to what I'm saying. I'll tell you the way it is. I'm the dispenser and not a receiver." Such implicit or explicit communications lead the other person to feel, "I don't exist for you. You need someone—anyone—to listen to you and to admire you. You don't need anything human from me as a person. You experience people as objects or ears or sexual partners only." This provokes anger and leads to ongoing distancing maneuvers, all of which serve to prevent any real human closeness or intimacy.

2. When there is a fear that "An unpleasant emotional reaction may occur if I speak up and respond to what is being said."

3. When there is a fear of involvement which may lead to intimacy or having one's territoriality and privacy intruded upon.

4. When there is a feeling of social unease, awkwardness, or ineptness.

5. When one of the communicants is such a "nit-picker" in interruptions for specific literal details that the speaker "loses" the point he was trying to make as well as the desire to complete his communication.

6. When one of the communicants feels so personally insignificant that he tends to be passive and rarely engages interactionally during dialogue.

55

Nonverbal Communications

When someone thumbs his nose at you, or smiles at you, or abruptly turns his back on you, you don't need a thousand-word speech to understand the feelings being expressed.

Nonverbal behaviors convey attitudes, cultural codes about how the present moment and situation are to be understood and, as Scheflen has so well stated in his writings, "serve to establish, maintain and regulate human relationships."[*]

Nonverbal behaviors may serve for expression, communication, or both:

1. They may express what we *consciously* wish to express and may do so in a concise and accurate manner. They may express what we consciously intend to express in the way of:

   anger—with a clenched fist;
   resentment—with a snarling face and gritted teeth;
   joy—with a happy, glowing smile;
   confusion—with a perplexed brow.

2. They may express what we *do not* consciously wish to express, and may ex-

press what we believe are secret or private thoughts or feelings. For example, the degree of a person's anxiety or tension in a conversation may be communicated by the way he smokes, e.g., by the frequency with which he lights cigarette after cigarette, by the rapid deep inhalations and powerful exhalations of smoke as he attempts to get rid of his "steam" or pent up tension, by the tightness of his wrist and fingers as he holds the cigarette, by the grinding fashion in which the cigarette is put out in the ashtray. Or a person who comes into a room where other people are gathered and hopes to appear calm and poised may stumble over his own feet or the edge of a rug, thus betraying his sense of tension and awkwardness.

Thus, we see that behaviors may express and reveal to others what is public and available to them, but is either known or unknown to ourselves about ourselves. For example, people who blush often are unaware of what they are doing until the other person says, "Hey, you're blushing—I didn't realize this would make you so un-

---

[*]Scheflen, Albert E.: "Communication and Regulation in Psychotherapy." *Psychiatry*, 26: 126-136, 1963.

comfortable." Or a man or woman may be sexually seductive in his/her body positioning or in his/her eyes without being aware of it, yet the seductive message is perceived and reacted to by others.

And various aspects of the personality of people we encounter in our daily life are telegraphed instantly to us as we look at them for the first time even though the senders are usually unaware of the powerful nonverbalized data they are sending and how much it establishes and regulates our relationship with them.

The commonality of recognition of nonverbal personality data is found in such everyday expressions as:

"He looked like a warm and friendly person so I immediately felt comfortable."

"You could feel at once he was an angry and bitter person who didn't like his job."

"Her eyes and smile showed her warmth and acceptance. I knew immediately where her children had gotten their trust and vitality from."

"I immediately felt safe and confident with him. He radiated a solid sense of confidence and knew just what to do."

"There was a glitter in her eyes which told me she was a woman who enjoyed life."

"His eyes were shifty, so I realized I'd better not trust him with too much of me."

"I could see the degree of agitation in him. He was taut like a drum. So, I moved very cautiously near him and spoke softly."

"I wasn't sure why, but I got very anxious when we met. There was something slippery or elusive about him."

"When I shook hands with him, I thought I was holding a dead fish. It gave me a weird feeling."

"I could tell immediately that she was a real woman and that she liked it."

"She reminded me of my mother. She was soft and accepting, and I felt comfortable throughout the interview."

"I could see from the way he looked at me that he is a man who had lived much pain and much joy and knows what life is all about. I liked him."

"He is a sparkling person. He has a glowing spirit."

"She has an honest face."

"He has a strong face."

Studies have shown that certain (not all) facial expressions are interpreted the same universally.° Eight pairs of emotion words reflecting facial expressions have been found to be accurately applied to photos showing clear-cut emotions by people in such diverse cultures as New Guinea, Japan, England, Brazil, Germany, Chile, Sweden, France, Greece, Africa, Hawaii, Turkey, and the United States. There was agreement in all these diverse cultures on facial expressions showing: (1) interest-excitement, (2) enjoyment-joy, (3) surprise-startle, (4) distress-anguish, (5) disgust-contempt, (6) anger-rage, (7) shame-humiliation, and (8) fear-terror.

In our work the evidence of a patient's progress is to be found nonverbally in: demeanor, attitude, gait, spirit, openness, spontaneity, capacity to give and receive, to listen with greater ease, to empathize, to enjoy, and to be realistic in behaviors.

°Ekman, Paul and Wallace, Freisen: "*Unmasking the Face,*" Prentice-Hall, Inc., New Jersey, 1975. The basic study by Charles Darwin in 1872 on *The Expression of the Emotions in Man and Animals* republished by Appleton Press in New York is must reading on this fascinating subject.

56

Roles
People Play

A role is a condensed name given to a cluster of repeated attitudes and behaviors which are characteristic of one's personality at certain times.

Becoming familiar with the self-defeating, self-isolating, and self-minimizing roles patients play over and over again allows you to more rapidly recognize them as they are being enacted or expressed. You can point these out to your patient (using good humored "I'm with you" mimicry at times) as you encourage patients towards more self-fulfilling roles. You can help patients understand the original basis and necessity for their having adopted such roles in childhood—for survival—while you simultaneously encourage them to give up what is now compulsive, inappropriate, and self-defeating.

Roles are portrayed through a series of simultaneous behaviors occurring and experienced together and triggering off a recognition process in the viewer(s) or interacting other(s). The role is expressed through non-verbal body position and posture, personality attitude, manner, and style; facial expressions; word interaction, speech pattern, accent rhythm; clothing, uniform, badges, jewelry or other adornments; grooming and other behaviors. The statement and portrayal through these and other means of one's role are calculated to establish, maintain and regulate the relationship between the role player and others in such a fashion that real feelings may be concealed or denied to oneself or others. Many people lose their real self or real identity in the belief that they really are the role they are playing.

The use of video replay with patients and others can often help them become more aware of how they express and communicate these roles verbally and nonverbally. Some of these roles are:[*]

JESTER	FLIRT
REFEREE-UMPIRE	SOPHISTICATE
CATALYST	COCKROACH
DON JUAN	TROUBLEMAKER
COCKTEASER	MAGICIAN
THE IDIOT	CHARMER
INJUSTICE COLLECTOR	ICONOCLAST
THE ABUSED TYPE	VICTIM
MISSIONARY	VINDICATOR
CRISIS CREATOR	PRIMA DONNA
STORY TELLER	FRAIL TYRANT
CLOCK-WATCHER	TEACHER'S PET
WHINER	PROSECUTOR
LEADER OF OPPOSITION	SEDUCER
NIT PICKER	GUARDHOUSE LAWYER
PLANNER	THE SCAPEGOAT
SELF-RIGHTEOUS CRITIC	REJECTION COLLECTOR
EXPERT	THE SAINT
PROVOCATEUR	FASHION PLATE
FRAGILE BABY	INNOCENT
GENERAL	ADVICE SEEKER
INTELLECTUAL	RUNT OF THE LITTER
VIRTUOUSLY HONEST SADIST	STRONG SILENT TYPE
OVERPROTECTIVE MAMA	COMPULSIVE HELPER
THE JUDGE	CAN'T SAY NO
KILL-JOY	MANIPULATOR
EGGHEAD	COMPETITOR
THE BAITER	OSTRICH
THE DOCTOR'S ASSISTANT	FAIR ONE
MARTYR	POLLYANNA
OMBUDSMAN-GUARDIAN	CASTRATOR
NEGATIVISTIC CLIQUE CREATOR	GUILT PROVOKER
HELP-REJECTING COMPLAINER	

[*]Berger, M.M.: The Use of Videotape in the Integrated Treatment of Individuals, Couples, Families and Groups in Private Practice, in Berger, M.M., Ed.: *Videotape Techniques in Psychiatric Training and Treatment.* New York: Brunner/ Mazel, Inc., 1970, pp. 138-9.

57   Exercises In Working With Patients

1. Find something to *praise* in all or almost all the patients you have contact with today—and say it to them. Incidentally, try to do the same with your fellow employees—and notice the results! Do this for one week and then see what differences exist in your relationship to your patients, to your fellow employees, and to yourself! These exercises on praise-giving can be best fulfilled through game-playing techniques.

2. The playing of *games* is a highly effective technique that helps stimulate:

    Interest

    Interpersonal communication

    Interaction

    Aliveness

    Involvement

    Intellectual exchanges

    Feelings of enjoying participating

    Feelings of enjoying contributing

    Cohesiveness

    Belonging

    Trusting

    Risk-Taking

3. Games in working with patients include:

Free-Association Games (for example, word games on universal topics such as fun, geographical places, or famous people)

Art-Expression Games (for example, one person starts a doodle and others add to it)

Fantasy Games* (for example, one person starts a story and others add to it)

Risk-Taking Games (for example, Monopoly, cards, checkers, chess)

Sensory Awareness and Expansion Games (for example, feel your face, your body, give yourself a hug, close your eyes and try to identify certain smells, such as herbs and spices)

Interpersonal Involvement Games (for example, have each person in the group say something positive to at least one other person in the group)

Self-Exposure Games (for example, express five nice things about yourself and then three things you don't like about yourself—and see if others feel about you as you do or differently)

Relaxation Games (for example, lean back in your chair and let your hands or feet just drop in a relaxed, effortless fashion)

Anxiety- and Fear-Reducing Games and Exercises (for example, think of a pleasant summer or place or experience from your childhood or past life while taking deep breaths and closing your eyes. This is often a good way to help people fall asleep)

4. Assertive Training to Acquire Emotionally Expressive Behaviors:

Learning to say "No"
Learning to say "Yes"
Learning to express affection, liking, anger
Learning to express sadness and fears
Learning to open conversation by expressing positive feelings to another person
Learning to be polite. Politeness doesn't have to be "stiff."

Once the appropriate overt expressions of emotions are learned, the inward or subjective feelings will be experienced —practice is required.

*Read A. Otto's *Fantasy Encounter Games.* Harper & Row, 1974.

58 Focus on Assets —Not Liabilities or Pathology

Help People Called Patients See the Glass as Half Full rather than Half Empty.

What are considered to be assets?

1. Health: Daily physical functioning and capacity to recover from prior illness (physical, emotional)

2. Appearance

3. Energy Available:
   Physical functioning under emotional stress
   Physical functioning under physical stress
   Emotional capacity to adapt to and function in stress situations

4. Functioning under influence of a reasonable amount of alcohol in social situations

5. I.Q.:
   Capacity to comprehend information or data available, and to obtain additional information required to draw an informed conclusion.
   Capacity to abstract and make connections between overt and covert causes and effects.

6. Family resources: Parents? Brothers? Sisters? Spouse? Children? Uncles? Aunts? Cousins? Others?

7. Friends: How many? Who? What is the degree of their interest and involvement with the patient?

8. Positive life experiences

9. Talents and Gifts:
    Music
    Art
    Athletic
    Writing
    Other (such as an awareness of the world in which the individual lives).

10. Skills and competency in daily living:
    Aptitude for abstract thinking (to "size up" a situation)
    Problem solving and capacity to make independent value judgments
    Understanding relationship between individual and environment
    Interpersonal relations: communicates clearly; projects personality in a positive manner and thus can relate well to others; can exert influence to bring about change in others' conclusions or behaviors
    Manual dexterity

11. Degree of common sense and appropriateness in daily living

12. Capacity for self control

13. Interest in working on self

14. Capacity to be introspective

15. Awareness of cultural opportunities and record of usage

16. Awareness of economic opportunities and financial assets and record of usage

17. Awareness of social opportunities and record of usage

18. Awareness of leisure time opportunities and record of usage

Think of additional resources and assets your patients, you and others may have. Get a large sheet of paper and list them in detail.

It's more important to recognize how healthy a patient is than how sick he/she is. The healthier you are, the more psychopathology or stress you can tolerate, learn to adapt to and recover from.

59 Dealing With Indecisiveness and Vacillation

Psychiatric patients are plagued with indecisiveness, and they tend to vacillate (back and forth) on many issues. This is often reflected in outward passivity, depression, and inertia, except for moments when they strike out inappropriately with words or actions expressing anger, rage, or frustration caused by or related to unresolved inner conflicts. Such frustration is often accompanied by anxiety, helplessness, hopelessness, and feelings of being alone in a hostile world.

Psychiatric patients generally function more compulsively than people without emotional or psychic disability. *All people have* emotional or psychic over-reactions, underreactions, or distortions, but not all people are so compulsively and insatiably driven to think, feel, or behave in ways which give themselves and others so much pain, unhappiness, and non-fulfillment as do the persons/clients seen by mental health workers.

The healthier a person is, the more capable he is of thinking of alternate choices, conjecturing upon their outcome, coming to grips with the pros and cons involved in conflict resolution, and then risking a new choice or option. Having or developing clearer values is a major aspect of conflict resolution and we can help clarify issues and values.

Decision-making and action-taking involve making choices after thinking of alternatives or options related to our values, wishes, and wants.

It is our task to:

1. Help patients fantasize (imagine or dream-up) or think about alternate possibilities and choices.

2. Help patients assess potential positive and negative results of each alternative or possibility.

3. Teach patients when it is healthier to stay with an unresolved situation (to be able to live in abeyance and not move into impulsive action) by developing an understanding of the concept of "masterful, purposeful inactivity."

4. Help patients see the positive strengths (*focus on assets*) in himself and his other resources which can enable him to risk a new way of functioning.

5. Clarify and help patients realize that some decisions have seemed impossible to make because the choice is not between what is "good or bad," "positive or negative," but rather between "what is the lesser of two evils?"

60 Some Common Symptoms/ Problems

There are certain symptoms, problems, and clusters of problems which occur repeatedly in persons suffering from different types of emotional and mental disorders. Many of these are accentuations of problems all of us have in daily living.' But our patients have not adequately learned how to face, accept, resolve, or cope with these problems, which then cause them much trouble. In helping people called patients to face and resolve or accept these in their integrated daily living, we reduce their anxiety, guilt, self-hate, and feelings of inadequacy, while increasing their sense of inner security and self-esteem.

Some of these symptoms/problems are:

1. Unresolved conflicts

2. Confusion

3. Helplessness

4. a) Anxiety—apprehension, tension, uneasiness stemming from an anticipated danger whose source is largely unknown or unrecognizable, with or without clear-cut body symptoms such as cardiac arrhythmias, rapid heartbeats, gastrointestinal distress, sweating, rashes, etc.

   b) Fears—of deep water, flying, loss of control, authorities, the opposite sex and so on and on.

   c) Phobias—obsessive, persistent, unrealistic fear of objects or situations like dirt, heights, open spaces, animals, touching.

5. Inability to feel or express anger

6. Difficulties in self-assertion

7. Passivity

8. Dependency

9. Depression

10. Hopelessness

11. Demoralization

12. Feeling stupid

13. Feeling inadequate

14. Alienation

15. Distancing patterns and arrangements

16. Help-rejecting complaining

17. Rejection collecting

18. Injustice collecting

19. Avoidance patterns

20. Resistance patterns

21. Self-defeating patterns and arrangements

22. Lack of self-esteem/self-worth/self-respect

23. Lack of self-confidence

24. Silences and absenting oneself from interpersonal involvements

25. Transferential allergies or overreactions to others

26. Emotional illiteracy—a deficit in repertoire of emotional feelings or capacity to identify and express feelings in words

27. Social ineptness or social hunger

28. Suspicion or distrust

29. Lack of impulse control

30. Problems in experiencing joy

31. Problems in giving and receiving

32. Repeated thoughts of suicide

33. Extreme self-hatred

34. Feeling abused

35. Repeated thoughts of harming others

36. Feeling empty

37. Identity confusion—a person may state, "I don't know who I am." This is a common cause for adolescent turmoil or crisis.

61 Sexual Behaviors In Psychiatric Settings

Covert sexually seductive behaviors and overt male-female relationships between inpatients create anxiety and confusion among mental health workers. Personnel are often plagued by conflict and inertia until acting-out occurs, usually as a result of lack of a clear-cut team, ward, unit, or institutional policy.

On the one hand, personnel may over-identify with a sexually inept or inexperienced patient, and may believe it is good for the patient to have an opportunity for experience, expression, practice, and, possibly, fulfillment of what is generally considered a maturing process. During inpatient courtships, previously difficult patients may be more manageable for the staff.

Such a situation and context may lead to personnel sending different, often contradictory, messages to patients. The basis for these highly charged, contradictory messages lies in the following factors:

1. Due to staff anxiety and uncertainty, there may be a gross denial of the situation.

2. Some staff members, still involved in their own adolescent rebellion against the "authorities," may collusively encourage and cooperate with the patients to some degree, living vicar-iously through them as they act out what is generally forbidden.

3. There may develop a compulsive over-interest in the "lovers," with their daily activities becoming the major subject of ward interest. The patients may, in fact, be "acting out" the sexual desires of the staff for their patients.

4. The staff may avoid using the experience to foster maturation by not emphasizing the importance of impulse control, frustration tolerance, and the concept of "appropriateness in behavior" as the basis for the art and skill of successful daily living.

In some institutions, there continues to be overt economic, physical, or sexual abuse of some patients by other patients. Before you are faced with such situations, it would be a good idea to talk with the other members of your treatment team about such behavior. You might also discuss the impact of sexual behavior among staff in front of patients, as well as sexual behavior between staff members and patients.

Can you become a facilitator or agent for change? Can you help others understand the process and impact of multilevel sexual communications (see pp. 95 to 104 on communications)?

62

No-No's For Staff

The *behaviors* of staff members in the presence of patients are important! They are observed both consciously and subliminally (outside of awareness), and reacted to in unpredictable fashions at unpredictable times. Following are some rules to keep in mind:

1. Don't talk about a patient in his presence with another staff member or family member unless you speak loud enough to include the patient in your interpersonal dialogue and interaction. Patients will strain to hear your "stage whispers," and will distort clear, let alone vague or partially heard, messages against themselves in a "paranoid" fashion. Most often they'll believe you are rejecting, criticizing, or planning to do something against them or their interests.

2. Don't carry on a sexual flirtation with another staff member in the presence of a patient.

3. Don't wear clothing or perfumes or behave in a manner which is so sexually provocative that the patient's sexual excitement and fantasy life are ex- tremely heightened. The context of institutional life is to be quieting and to offer normalizing stimuli. Extra difficulties in controlling sexual impulses triggered in patients by staff members may lead to acting-out sexually with other patients who are also particularly vulnerable during periods of emotional disturbance. This often is followed by restrictions which are experienced as punitive and lead to further acting-out.

4. Don't buffoon or clown around in the presence of a suffering patient. While a sense of humor is valuable in our work, it is important that your expression of humor be *appropriate* in content, timing and context.

5. Don't lead the patient to believe you are ignoring his presence or existence since that further augments his feeling of being an object—a "nothing."

6. Don't shout at or argue with patients. Such an approach is not only antitherapeutic, usually, but *it may provoke a violent reaction towards you!*

7. Don't enter into collusive schemes or business arrangements with patients.

8. Don't loan money to patients. Such an arrangement heightens dependency and is just not realistic. Your task is to provide human help and guidance, *not* to subsidize or finance patients.

9. Don't go beyond your scope and expertise in trying to advise or guide patients. If your advice is wrong, it is the patient who has to pay the price for the mistake—not you. When in doubt as to what to say or do, suggest that the patient talk to his or her therapist.

63 Self-Defeating Aspects Of Neurotic Functioning

The development of neurotic trends was a necessity for the individual's survival as a defense against fears, angers, aloneness, confusion, annihilation, and other unclear feelings which are difficult to express during childhood and adolescent years. However, in our adult years such neurotic functioning wastes energies (that could be used more creatively and productively) by directing them into security operations characterized by the fact that they are compulsive (not freely chosen), inappropriate, exaggerated, and insatiable.

The following list of aspects of neurotic functioning allows us to "focus in" on specific areas and systems as we work psychotherapeutically and re-educationally with people called patients.

1. Functioning is driven/compulsive—based on "shoulds" not "wants."

2. Insatiability—"never enough"—may appear as greediness (for affection or material things).

3. Disproportionate response—(a) over-reactions due to over-identification, hypersensitivity to criticism, transferential "allergies" to people; (b) under-reactions due to blind spots, denials, or the need to please or be liked.

4. Measuring one's functioning in relation to an idealized image rather than reality.

5. Need to be perfect—excessive expectations of self and others.

6. Frequently feeling angry or guilty with self for not measuring up to excessive expectations of self or internalized expectations from others.

7. Proving rather than improving.

8. Impressing rather than expressing.

9. Either/or functioning—good or bad, right or wrong, succeeding or failing —due to compartmentalizing or having rigid values.

10. Need to control—an attempt to create an illusion of security in an uncertain world.

11. Lack of spontaneity—reduced awareness and aliveness of feeling, as well as reduced capacity for expression.

12. An inappropriateness of feelings, thought, or behavior.

13. A lack of wholeheartedness—(a) an inability to be into what one is into with the whole of oneself; (b) an inability to be fully committed.

14. A difficulty in adapting to changing situations, especially stressful ones, due to rigidity of functioning and compulsiveness.

15. Inertia—a paralysis of initiative and action due to idealized image.

16. Ineffectiveness—caused by our energies being pushed and pulled in conflictual directions.

17. Indecisiveness—an inability to make choices and to accept their consequences.

18. Incapacity to assume adequate responsibility for oneself in some areas of life—inability to feel oneself the active, responsible force in one's life.

19. Lack of inner independence—an inability to establish one's own values and apply them to actual living.

20. Inability to recognize, express, and act on options.

21. Fear of risk-taking.

22. More or less experiencing of "basic anxiety"—which Karen Horney[*] defines as "the feeling of being isolated and helpless in a world conceived as potentially hostile. A wide range of adverse factors in the environment can produce this insecurity in a child: direct or indirect domination, indifference, erratic behavior, lack of respect for the child's individual needs, lack of real guidance, disparaging attitudes, too much admiration or the absence of it, lack of reliable warmth, having to take sides in parental disagreements, too much or too little responsibility, overprotection, isolation from other children, injustice, discrimination, unkept promises, hostile atmosphere, so on and so on."

[*]Horney, K., *Our Inner Conflicts*, p. 41, New York: W. W. Norton and Company, 1945.

64

Who and What Is a Person?

A person is a process of sub-systems and of many selves in continuing motion—always changing, yet trying to remain "stable" or "balanced" in homeostasis.

I, as an individual, am . . .

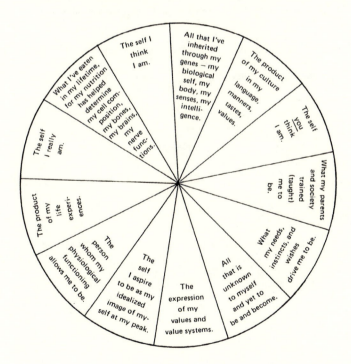

The self I think I am.

All that I've inherited through my genes — my biological self, my body, my senses, my intelligence.

The product of my culture in my language, manners, tastes, values.

The self you think I am.

What my parents and society trained (taught) me to be.

What my needs, instincts, and wishes drive me to be.

All that is unknown to myself and yet to be and become.

The expression of my values and value systems.

The self I aspire to be as my idealized image of myself at my peak.

The person whom my physiological functioning allows me to be.

The product of my life experiences.

The self I really am.

What I've eaten in my lifetime, for my nutrition has helped determine my cell composition, my bones, my brains, my nerve functions.

Some more or less fixed aspects of a person are name, height, skin color, body build, sex, language, accent, cultural background, inherited qualities, and much more.

A 28-year-old single female who has lived her life to please others and lives her life in such a way that she will make no waves recently described herself as *all* of the following:

honest	sincere	lovely
charming	a lady	scared
fat	incompetent	lazy
sloppy	vivacious	trustworthy
confident	inferior	not capable
efficient	witty	dull
serious	easygoing	good natured
depressed	moody (fairly)	attractive
complacent	ambitious	not disciplined
defensive	open	candid
lonely	love-starved	a bullshitter
arrogant	dizzy	highfalutin
up in the clouds	not realistic	impressionable
indecisive	winsome	unpassionate
understanding	likeable	

This example gives some notion as to the complexity of the many aspects of "self" or "inner selves" which make up an individual "self" or person.

65 Statements Indicating Depression

An assessment of depression in patients is based on high frequency of statements like:

"I feel downhearted and blue."

"I have trouble sleeping."

"I can't get interested in anything."

"I don't have much appetite these days."

"I have crying spells or feel like crying most of the time."

"I notice that I'm losing weight."

"I have trouble with constipation."

"I don't feel like getting up in the morning."

"I get tired and restless for no reason."

"At times I'm restless and agitated and don't know what to do with myself."

"I'm more irritable than I used to be."

"I don't enjoy anything anymore."

"Sex? I couldn't care less."

"I feel no one needs me anymore."

"I feel that I'm a burden—and others would be better off if I were dead."

"I just don't feel anything—I'm numb."

"At times I just wish I was dead."

66 A Dialogue With a Suicidal Patient

Don't deny or ignore the patient's feelings. *Do* help him see it's only a portion of his total self he wants to get rid of!

It is quite common for emotionally or mentally ill patients, the majority of whom suffer with some degree of acute or chronic depression, to express thoughts of suicide or to wish for death.

In almost all instances, I have found that what works is to help the potentially suicidal patient realize that he is wishing for or wanting the death of his *whole self* in order to get rid of a *part* or *aspect of himself* which he finds so *raw, painful, despicable, shameful,* or *hateful* that it seems impossible to go on living unless this *raw, painful, despicable, shameful,* or *hated* self is disposed of.

Step 1: I first ask: "Do you know what there is in you that you can't live with?" (or "that you find so intolerable or painful?" or "that you've got to get rid of?").

   Typical responses are: "I can't live with my guilt," "I can't face my family because of what I've done," "I'm such a nothing, I fail at everything I do and cause nothing but pain to everyone."

Step 2: I then say: "This is only part of you. You are more than your guilt" (or "You are more than your failures").

Step 3: Having introduced the concept that the patient is a whole person who is more than the part of him or her he cannot tolerate and wishes to kill off, I offer to help him become clearer about these two parts of himself, the unacceptable and the acceptable.

Step 4: I work to have the patient become clearer and to own all those parts of "self" which are worthwhile and worthy of respect and "love." I engage him in figuring out ways he can be different or feel different about what is so unacceptable.

Step 5: I do not attempt to simplify, whitewash, minimize, or deny the patient's belief in the validity of his judgment as to his situation and the correctness of his conclusion, i.e., that his only solution is to kill himself. But I do attempt to help relieve and alter his *totally condemning concept* of himself as a "failure," as "unworthy to live." I help him to examine the context or background of his life—of the events leading to the present situation. I help him to understand and then, hopefully, to accept that: "Such as I am I can only do the best I can do," or "In view of my family life, life circumstances, education, and opportunities, I only did the best I could do then."

I help the patient to become responsible for that which he is responsible for—but without perpetuating guilt or self-blame. If it is true that "such as I was, I could only do the best I could do. After all even I could not do the impossible!"—then he can begin to be less total in this self-condemnation and less vindictive. Once massive, overwhelming guilt and self-hate are reduced, the patient can be helped to see the unreasonableness of his past and present expectations. *He can learn that he, like all others, cannot expect what he has or had only a right to hope for!*

Step 6: More reasonable and appropriate values and self-judgment systems can be introduced to the patient as he acknowledges that it would be foolish to have killed off his total self permanently in order to get rid of a part or aspect of his self-image or self-concept which was undesirable because of excessive expectations of himself which came from others as well as himself.

Step 7: He can now move towards clarifying, developing and working towards more reasonable goals! He can give up excessive expectations, too!

The patient drawn to believe or act on his belief that the only way out of his painful dilemma is to commit suicide needs to learn that there may be another choice open to him. Initially he feels he has no other choice or option. In the process of maintaining a dialogue with a potentially suicidal person, it is sometimes of help to make comments such as: "Well, if you do kill yourself it will be your responsibility. You can't expect others to feel guilty. They may feel *bad* but *they don't have to feel guilty!*" "I'd certainly feel bad to see the waste and loss of a person like you through such a self-destructive choice. You certainly are worth caring for and about. I care and I'd feel bad—not guilty." You can influence people who think about or even have made a suicidal attempt to give up their suicidal ruminations, wishes, and plans.

In working with potentially suicidal patients *we need to continually assess and re-assess:*

1. How serious is the patient in his or her intent? How much preoccupation with ideas and thoughts and images concerning suicide? What specific kinds of ideas? Are plans being formulated? Is there reading on the subject going on? Is he or she setting a specific date?

2. Have there been prior attempts at suicide? How lethal was each attempt? (Swallowing 15 aspirins has a different implication than 15 sleeping pills prescribed by a physician.)

3. Does the patient have a chronic disease?

4. Does the patient live alone?

5. Does the patient talk to anyone—or keep feelings bottled up inside?

6. Are there other specific evidences of not caring for self?

7. Does this patient hear "command voices" saying "Kill yourself"?

8. Are there any provocative elements in

this setting that could trigger a suicidal attempt? This means people (including staff and other patients), as well as objects like belts, knives, razors, and poisonous cleaning materials.

9. Are there any pending visits to or from disturbing relatives or others? This is more likely on a weekend.

10. Is the patient cooperating in our efforts to help him or her avoid committing suicide?

11. Does this patient still maintain fairly good self-control?

67

What Is
Drug Addiction?

Drug addiction is a compulsive, repeated craving for certain substances which, when taken into the body, temporarily alleviate certain painful, disturbing feelings, thoughts, or perceptions, or serve to induce a more pleasurable state of euphoria which is anxiety-freeing.

A very strong emotional and physiological dependence is present in addicts, resulting in a need for larger and larger doses of the addictive substance. While there is no one personality type or family background which spawns the "addict," there is almost always an immature personality, a low level of frustration tolerance and impulse control, a disturbance in reality testing, and a tendency to seek magical solutions for life's problems.

We know that individuals—mostly younger people in our society—turn to drugs for one or more of the following:

1. *To move away from feelings* such as pain, anxiety, self-hate, boredom, loneliness, confusion, feeling "lost" or helpless, being "hassled," or growing up.

2. *To move toward* escape, joy, happiness, freedom from awareness of pain or responsibility, excitement, fantasies.

An addict states, "I took drugs because it allowed me to feel open as if I were flowing and flying. I liked the feeling of freedom to fly with no resistance, no restraints, no constraints. I like to just have feelings, to just have sensations and no thoughts to bother me. I like not having to be serious."

In working with addicts, there are certain common problems we try to help them and their families with. Some of these are:

1. The need to examine and give up excessive dependency needs.

2. The need to give up an attitude and behavior which state not only that, "I want what I want when I want it," but also "and its coming to me." Addicts need to learn what "reality" and "growing up" are about, and what the positive rewards are which come from *"postponing present pleasure for future profit."*

3. The need to build up their capacity to tolerate and live with impulse-control, frustration, ambiguity, inner conflict, anxiety, as well as "trust."

4. The need to develop a better self-image and an awareness of "self."

125

5. The need to develop a respect for inner and outer structure, rules and rational authority.

Unfortunately many people have become addicted to hard drugs, barbiturates, amphetamines and other substances after first being introduced to these materials in therapeutic prescriptions. We must learn to recognize signs of craving and excessive demand as well as the signs of over-dosage in our patients. We should not prescribe more of anything than the patient really needs and in amounts which will lead us to review the patient's medications frequently.

There are similar dynamics involved in all addictions, including alcoholism.

68 Some Basic Concepts Of Psychodynamics

Psychodynamics is concerned with understanding the motives of human behavior. Some basic concepts are:

1. Symptoms have meaning—they not merely give us information to make a differential diagnosis but also offer us motivational and etiological clues and meanings.

2. Human behavior is motivated and can be understood, although it is a difficult task. It is easier to understand what has occurred than to predict what will occur. This is also true of psychopathological behavior. There is a value for every human behavior even though that value may be in the service of supporting a neurotic, psychotic, or destructive system.

3. In making psychodynamic interpretations, one's inferences as to motive or value may be correct or incorrect or partially correct according to the soundness of one's concepts of motivation, the adequacy of one's information, and one's skill in drawing inferences of this kind.

4. The same behavior may be interpreted differently from different theoretical viewpoints (Freud, Jung, Adler, Horney, transactional analysis, commonsense, etc.). Each different interpretation may have some partial validity.

5. There continue to be conflict and discussion on the general subject of "determinism." Some feel almost everything is predetermined and others feel little is predetermined. Most people today do agree that the events of early childhood, plus general social, educational, and economic circumstances and opportunities, as well as family values, attitudes, communications and relationships, constitute clear and unclear forces which shape the general course of our personality development. They also form the basis for our value judgments and, therefore, our motivational pressures which guide or constrain us as we grow older on our journey through experiencing and adventuring through risk-taking toward security, success, and self-esteem—or toward failure and self-hate. Behavior is also influenced by our physiological functioning, as well as by pathological changes. Great differences of potentialities and limitations exist in different people.

6. The understanding of the process of human behavior has been helped considerably by the clarification of concepts called Mental Mechanisms (see next chapter) which occur in almost all people in all cultures at different times. I refer here to such concepts as sublimation, displacement, repression, projection or externalization, internalization or incorporation, magical thinking, rationalization, etc.

Many psychotherapeutic and associated non-medicinal treatment approaches utilize some or all of these psychodynamic concepts. They may be practiced with individuals, couples, families or with small or large groups. Some of these treatment approaches are:

Psychoanalysis

Psychoanalytically oriented psychotherapy

Brief psychotherapy

Psychoanalytically oriented art, movement, music, and poetry therapy

Gestalt therapy

Transactional analysis

Psychodrama

Behavior therapy

Non-directive therapy

Rational therapy

Biofeedback

Bioenergetic therapy

Sex therapy

69

Mental Defense Mechanisms

Some common psychic mechanisms used to defend oneself against painful and unpleasant feelings, thoughts, or conflicts are listed here. While all of these are necessary at times in everyday living and are used by reasonably well-functioning individuals, we find that mentally ill persons use these mechanisms too much of the time, and thus avoid maturing and living in reality to the degree healthier, actualized, and more fulfilled persons do.

ABSENTING ONESELF—Tuning out to avoid hearing or seeing what is painful or otherwise intolerable at a specific moment in relationships with others.

AMNESIA—Forgetting significant data or events which are too painful to live with consciously.

COMPENSATION—Because of deep-seated feelings of inferiority and inadequacy, there is an unconscious attempt by the individual to defend himself with measures designed to increase self-esteem and attain a sense of security. *Normally,* the compensatory mechanism will manifest itself in greatly accelerated strivings for suc-

cess or acclaim on a realistic level. *Morbidly,* compensation may express itself in terms of excessive daydreaming, wishful thinking and fantasy without action, aggressive and overly assertive behavior and character traits, and psychotic delusions.

CONDENSATION—This represents the compression of several unconscious wishes, impulses, thoughts, or objects into a single conscious image, thought, word, act, or symptom.

CONVERSION—The expression of unconscious psychic conflicts through physical symptoms which often have a symbolic relationship to the unconscious (repressed) conflict.

DENIAL—Unacceptable wishes, impulses, feelings, and thoughts, as well as external realities, are unconsciously repudiated and ignored by the individual as if they did not exist.

DISPLACEMENT—The transposition of feelings unconsciously associated with an individual, object, or event to an indifferent or innocuous substitute on the conscious level, with the original focus remaining unconscious. This occurs often in phobias and in compulsive neuroses.

DISSOCIATION—A segment of the unconscious which is producing intense emotional conflict is segregated away from the main personality structure and functions separately. This may lead to conditions such as fugue states, automatic writing, somnambulism, amnesia, and dual or multiple personalities.

DISTORTING—Altering real people, ideas, memories, situations, and things so that they are not accurately presented to self or others (see redefining process, page 55).

EVADING—Use of disguises, compartmentalizing, fabrications, blind spots, and denials to avoid facing truths or being faced with responsibility which is not wanted or cannot be lived up to.

MAGICAL THINKING—Developing or perpetuating a belief that through some magical means problems will be solved; painful, difficult, or reality situations will disappear and not have to be confronted responsibly. This is a perpetuation of a process which begins in childhood.

IDEALIZATION—Marked overevaluation of a loved object.

IDEALIZED IMAGE FORMATION— Refers to the development and perpetuation of an ideal self-concept which is used to drive a person so that he will feel good when he comes momentarily towards achieving the demands of his image.

IDENTIFICATION—An individual unconsciously attaches to himself certain elements or qualities associated with someone else, because he wishes to be like the other person (positive identification). Or else the mental image of someone in the past who roused painful or unpleasant emotions is transferred to a current surrogate figure who consequently evokes the same emotions (hostile identification). An example of the latter would be resentment toward all authority figures who represent a feared, tyrannical father.

INCORPORATION OR INTROJECTION—The image of another person is incorporated within the unconscious, with all the emotions and the sentiments surrounding this other person. The mechanism may be used for identification, to be like the incorporated object, or for the destruction of the object. Introjection to destroy a once-loved object is found in certain severe depressions and may result in suicide.

ISOLATION—The separation of an idea from its attending emotion, with the idea admitted to conscious awareness while the emotion remains unconscious, repressed. This is observed frequently in obsessive-compulsive neurotics.

PROJECTION—The individual attributes to others his own unconscious unacceptable wishes, impulses, feelings, and motives.

REACTION FORMATION—An unconscious, painful, or undesirable character trait or attitude is covered up by the conscious presentation of a fixed, rigid trait or attitude of an opposite nature. For example, excessive amiability may be the reaction formation to disguise unconscious hostility.

RATIONALIZATION—Excuses or reasoning designed to explain in a favorable way behavior or attitudes arising from unconscious motives.

REGRESSION—When unable to cope with internal or external pressures, the individual reverts to an earlier or more infantile level of behavior and gratification.

REPRESSION—Unbearable wishes, impulses, tendencies and desires painful to the ego are pushed into the unconscious, where they cannot be recovered by the ordinary process of voluntary recall. Repression accounts for many people's amnesia covering early painful events and circumstances.

SUBLIMATION—Deep, infantile instinctual energies are changed in form and aim so that an individual can express, channel, and gratify his inhibited instincts in more socially acceptable ways as he matures and is more influenced by his ego and superego.

70

Patients'
Bill Of Rights

To be able to:

1. Communicate with persons outside the facility via correspondence, telephone, and visits

2. Keep clothing and personal effects

3. Have religious freedom

4. Vote

5. Be employed if possible

6. Manage or dispose of property

7. Execute instruments such as wills

8. Enter contractual relationships

9. Make purchases

10. Obtain education

11. Seek habeas corpus

12. Have an independent psychiatric examination

13. Gain civil service status

14. Retain licenses, privileges, or permits established by law

15. Sue or be sued

16. Marry

17. Not be subject to unnecessary mechanical restraints

This is a summary of the detailed rights of patients as presented in a booklet entitled "Patients' Rights" published by the American Psychiatric Association in 1975 and in accordance with the principles outlined in the Accreditation Manual for Psychiatric Facilities 1972, published by Joint Commission on Accreditation of Hospitals, 645 North Michigan Avenue, Chiacgo, Ill. 60611.

The 1975 Mental Hygiene Law of New York State has some detailed specific components of quality of care and treatment for the mentally disabled. Some provisions of the law are that:

"Patients have a right to an individual program of services which will maximize their abilities to cope with their environment, will foster social and vocational competence and will enable them to live as independently as possible.

"Patients have a right to be treated in a way which acknowledges and respects their cultural identity.

"Patients have a right to a maximum amount of privacy consistent with the effective delivery of services. This includes, but is not restricted to, privacy of person, of personal belongings, and of communications.

"Patients have a right to object to any

form of care or treatment and to appeal decisions with which they disagree.

"Directors and staff of facilities shall provide services for mental disability in such a manner that patients receive care and treatment that is suited to their needs and skillfully, safely and humanely administered with full respect for their dignity and personal integrity.

"The staff of facilities shall employ restraint and seclusion only when absolutely necessary to protect the patient from injuring himself or herself or others." It adds that restraint or seclusion is a "procedure which shall be ordered by a physician and the facts and reasons for its use set forth." Records must be kept subject to inspection by authorized persons showing orders signed from day to day by a physician. "For seclusion these orders shall be rewritten daily and only after a personal examination by a physician."

Certain institutional practices diminish the sense of being human.° Institutional and individual approaches which diminish the patient's already decreased or low sense of identity, positive self-concept, and self-esteem include:

1. The loss of personal clothes, books, keys, money, identification cards, credit cards, pens, pencils, cigarette lighter or matches, and other nonhuman objects or possessions after entry into a psychiatric hospital, where one is stripped of clothes and forced to wear institutional clothing.

2. Being called or referred to by an identifying number rather than by name.

3. Being called by first name ("Mary," rather than "Mrs. Miller") without having been asked if that's OK, or being referred to as "Hey you!"

4. Being so crowded in with others that there is little or no personal space.

5. Being forced to evacuate one's bowels or bladder in a very limited time in the toilet—to do it on demand, so to speak.

6. Using a toilet with no door (and sometimes with no seat) while exposed to others' toilet sounds, smells and views.

7. Being denied access to a personal closet or drawers in which to place a few personal possessions, whether they be a bar of soap, a comb, toilet water, a letter, or a magazine.

8. Being deprived of an opportunity to receive mail or to make a telephone call.

9. Being threatened, punished, or otherwise abused or deprived for expressing anger in anger-provoking situations.°°

°Erving Goffman, *Essays on the Social Situation of Mental Patients and Other Inmates,* New York: Doubleday & Co., 1961.
°°See the movie *One Flew Over the Cuckoo's Nest* starring Jack Nicholson.

71 The Right To Treatment— Or To Refuse It

Human and civil rights have come into major focus in the 30 years since the holocaust executed against humanity by Hitler and his dictator companions before and during World War II.

In the 1960's, the attorney David N. Fields of New York City was instrumental in bringing about the release of incarcerated, untreated persons at Mattawean State Hospital who had been held in a maximum security institution while neither properly committed for or receiving psychiatric treatment nor actually convicted for committing a crime against society. The discharge of prisoners from Mattawean to other state hospitals for observation and disposition led to most such persons being discharged back into society after years of being deprived of their civil rights and freedom while warehoused in the most debilitating of institutions.

In 1963, when I examined a young man of 33 who had been at Mattawean for 18 years for having threatened to harm a liquor store dealer who sold liquor to his alcoholic mother, I found him non-psychotic and quite able to recall that he'd been sent to Mattawean because he was confused when brought before a judge after his arrest. He was now an emotionally,

intellectually and financially impoverished, alienated Simple-Simon-like institutionalized victim who reminded me of some lobotomized patients I'd seen years earlier. Having lost his spirit and his capacity for joy or fantasy or curiosity, he was "beat."

As attention focused on those persons warehoused for decades in state hospitals throughout our country, a few cases were brought to the state and federal courts. What emerged was the "right to treatment" concept which has been declared valid from Alabama and Florida all the way to New York and Alaska!

The American Psychiatric Association announced in July 1975 its definition of the right to treatment as beginning with a definition of "adequate care and adequate treatment."

"Adequate care requires the availability of adequate shelter in an uncrowded and pleasant setting, opportunities for recreational and vocational activities, and protection from self and others. These aspects of care should be incorporated in a total environment which is compatible with basic human comfort and dignity. This environment should be only as restrictive of personal liberty as is necessary to protect and meet the needs of the patient and society.

"Assurance that adequate treatment is available is best achieved by assuring the availability of a medical and allied health professional staff which is adequate in numbers and training.

"Treatment should include active intervention of a psychological, biological, physical, chemical, educational, moral or social nature, where the application of the individual treatment plan is felt to have a reasonable expectation of improving the patient's condition."

The APA stressed the fact that the right to adequate care and adequate treatment should be recognized for all hospitalized patients whether voluntarily or involuntarily committed. Once this right is recognized and adequate financial resources are provided and utilized, the specific care and treatment plan for each individual patient is a clinical matter to be determined by the responsible mental health professional, subject to suitable review.

The APA further states that "recognition of a definition of a right to adequate care and treatment implies *that society through its agencies* has a duty to implement and enforce this right. It would be unjust and unreasonable for courts to hold psychiatrists personally and individually responsible for resource deficiencies which are actually the responsibility of society."

The Right to Refuse Treatment

The American Psychiatric Association, in publishing its recent (1975) position on the right of patients to refuse treatment,° stated, "Except in emergencies, if a patient who is competent to participate in treatment decisions declines to accept treatment recommended by staff, we accept the patient's right to refuse. If the physician believes the patient is not competent to participate in treatment decisions, he should ask a court to rule on the patient's competency. . . . In cases where the patient refuses treatment which is deemed essential by the medical staff, and where this refusal is supported by the judiciary, the medical staff should review whether his right to care should be implemented in another facility."

°Herndon, Alma. "APA declares support for Right to Treatment," *Psychiatric News*, July 16, 1975, Vol. 10, No. 14, p. 1.

72 An Overview Of Community Psychiatry

Community psychiatry refers to the provision by a psychiatric center and its own satellite units, working in liaison with other providers of services in the catchment area which it serves, of (1) education and prevention; (2) crisis intervention; (3) outpatient and inpatient treatment with psychotropic medications, psychotherapy with individuals, couples, families, and groups; (4) vocational, social and activity, educational, rehabilitational approaches and other guidance and counseling as required.

Community psychiatry embraces all modalities of therapy and rehabilitation in outpatient clinics, partial day hospitals, sheltered workshops, halfway houses and other residential and nursing homes, as well as inpatient centers in specifically psychiatric hospitals or in general hospitals. Its administrative professionals and nonprofessional staff regularly meet with and are responsive to community boards composed of consumers as well as providers of services in the area served by the community mental health center (CMHC).

Community Psychiatry From 4 Points of View

Prevention

Planned Parenthood
Genetic Counseling Centers
Prenatal Care and Clinics
Sex Education Programs, In
Churches, Elementary
and High Schools,
College and Professional
Schools, Especially to
Medical Students and
Nurses
School Integration
Programs
Contraception and Abortion
Guidance and Clinics
Well Baby Clinics and
Pediatric Service
Nursery Schools and Child
Day Care Centers
Child Study Association
Workshops, Seminars
P.T.A. Workshops,
Lectures, Involvement in
Their Children's School
Programs
Society for Prevention of
Cruelty to Children

Outpatient Services

Child Abuse Treatment
Programs
School Guidance
Counseling
Consultation Services to
Welfare, Police

Child Guidance Bureau of
Board of Education
Sensitivity Groups for
Teachers
Special Services for
Children with Learning
Disabilities
Industrial Psychiatry
Mental Health Clinics
Walk-In Treatment Centers
Pastoral Counseling
Encounter and Sensitivity
Groups
Parent and Family
Counseling, Treatment
Centers
Suicide Prevention
Programs
Legal Aid Services
Psychiatric Consultants in
Schools and Courts
Drug Abuse Prevention
Programs
Big Brother Programs
Homemaker Services
Sex Treatment Centers
Partial Hospitalization
Units
Rap Sessions
Outreach Programs
Alcoholics Anonymous
Mobile Crisis Units
Drug Therapy
Family Doctors
Communal Living Hotels
and Apartments
Family and Home Visits
Mental Retardation Special
Programs
Emergency Room Crisis
Centers

Inpatient Services

Short Term Hospitalization
Programs
Hospitalization of Varying
Duration
Multi-Family Treatment
Groups
Family Group Treatment
Daily Living Groups
Social Welfare Services
Patient Government
Therapeutic Community
Psychiatric Consultation on
Medical Surgical Services
Residential Drug Treatment

Aftercare and Rehabilitation Services

Rehabilitation Services
Sheltered Workshops
Work for Pay Programs
Day Centers
Vocational Guidance and
Training
Transitional Job Placement
Halfway Houses
Nursing Homes
Foster Home Programs
Aftercare Clinics
Adult Education Groups
Self-Help Groups
Recovery, Inc.
Therapeutic Social Clubs

COMMUNITY PSYCHIATRY 137

73

Mental Health Career Definitions

Here are some things you might want to know about people working in this field.

1.   A *psychiatrist* is first of all a medical doctor who has had years of postgraduate training in learning how to examine, evaluate, diagnose, and treat people who are referred to as having emotional and/or mental illnesses or disorders. Because of his knowledge of human anatomy and physiology, both in health and in sickness, he is able to know the *effects* of various kinds of medications on people and, incidentally, is licensed to prescribe them. He also has had specific training in diseases of the nervous system and can, therefore, differentiate between organic brain diseases (due to tumors, alcohol, syphilis, Huntington's chorea, etc.), dysfunctions of the mind which are due to mental or emotional causes, and psychiatric disability due to such physical reasons as hyperthyroidism, anemias, cerebral vasospasm, etc. He often is the one to integrate the contributions of each member of the treatment unit.

2.   A *psychologist* is a person who has specialized in the field of clinical psychology, testing, or research, and has a graduate academic degree (Ph.D. or M.A.). Some people with a Bachelor of Arts degree in Psychology work as psychologists under supervision in varied settings. Psychologists are trained in how mind perception, intelligence, behavior, and personality develop, as well as in administering and interpreting various types of tests (Rorschach, Wechsler-Bellevue, Hartford-Shipley, etc.) to determine intellectual and mental functioning and impairment. In many areas, their knowledge overlaps that of psychiatrists, particularly when both groups have been trained specifically in the science and art of psychotherapy. They are not licensed to prescribe medications. They may hold certificates to practice in most states.

3.   A *psychoanalyst* is a psychiatrist, psychologist, social worker, or other mental health professional who has satisfactorily completed a supervised training program, which also included a personal psychoanalysis, leading to certification as a practitioner of psychoanalysis. Such certification leads to eligibility for membership in the American Academy of Psychoanalysis or the American Psychoanalytic Association or their equivalents in other countries. Certified psychoanalysts know the theories and techniques of psychoanal-

ysis and can appropriately employ these techniques for deep personality and character reconstruction in persons considered suitable for this form of psychotherapy.

4. A *psychiatric social worker* is a social worker who has had training and experience in one or more of the special fields of psychiatry and who has achieved a Master of Social Work Degree (M.S.W.) or is a certified social worker (C.S.W.), having passed certain examinations attesting to knowledge of the impact of sociological, familial, environmental, cultural, and economic forces on individuals and families. Many psychiatric social workers also specialize in what is called "group work," which actually overlaps with the fields of "group dynamics" and "group therapy." When trained in the art and science of psychotherapy, social workers work in a parallel fashion to psychiatrists and psychologists. Social workers are colleagues in developing and practicing one or more of the many types of psychotherapy and counseling available today.° (See Chapter 68 on concepts of psychodynamics.) They usually work as part of a team.

5. A *psychiatric nurse* is a registered nurse (R.N.) who has had graduate-level education and clinical experience in working with mentally and emotionally ill patients in psychiatric inpatient or outpatient settings. She is trained to integrate the data of the body as well as emotions and mind in applying her previously learned nursing skills. Psychiatric nurses usually work as part of a team.

6. *Rehabilitation specialists* are divided into a number of distinct categories and specialties:

Activities therapists: These are indi-viduals trained in the skilled use of various creative modalities, including art, dance, music, poetry, and their clinical applications for assessment and treatment of individuals and groups. In general, they are trained at a postgraduate level and registered through professional assocations.

Occupational therapists are specialized in activities therapy through undergraduate or graduate training programs, and are additionally trained in areas of remotivation, the teaching of self-care and independent management skills. While O.T.'s customarily meet uniform professional standards and are professionally registered, certified occupational therapy assistants and non-certified personnel trained through combinations of education and experience often fulfill parts of the roles of occupational therapists.

Recreation therapists are activities specialists who most typically utilize the structure of formal or informal games and planned social events to mobilize patients, afford resocializing experiences, and help build valid leisure pursuits. Training typically includes college preparation in physical recreation and/or related training and human service experience.

Rehabilitation counselors are prepared through graduate training in psychology, assessment, medical aspects of mental and physical impairments, and social and vocational development to plan and coordinate individual and group services to restore individuals to fuller and more independent functioning. Training typically consists of the Master's Degree in Rehabilitation Counseling, and professional certification in rehabilitation counseling. Rehabilitation counseling emphasizes short-term, intermediate, and long-range

---

°Individual psychoanalysis, analytically-oriented brief or long-term individual, couple, family, or group psychotherapy, transactional, Gestalt, behavioral or psychodramatic therapy, individual or group educational, vocational or rehabilitative counseling, etc.

goal-oriented planning to restore capacities for social participation, physical functioning, independent living, and occupation. Personnel with related experience and training often fulfill portions of the rehabilitation counselor's role, including, for example, vocational placement.

7. *Mental health therapy aides and assistants* are perhaps the most important members of the entire inpatient treatment team because they are in the closest contact with patients. They reflect the attitudes of the entire treatment team. The role of the aide will continue to grow in significance as the aide moves from serving as a custodian of warehoused persons to an active remotivational, educational, and rehabilitative team member. Such a development can be expedited as aides are involved in the preparation of training manuals and audiovisual materials.

All of these people are members of the treatment team. At times they work similarly in their approach to patients.

At other times each brings his own special skills and background to his or her unique approach to each patient. When they work together with consensus as a team—amplifying one another's efforts— they provide the best foundation for the care and treatment of patients and their families.

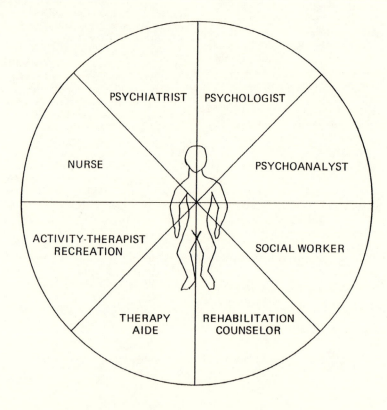

74 Job Titles Of Mental Health Paraprofessionals

Some of the training program and job titles currently used by mental health paraprofessionals are:

Mental Health Aide

Mental Health Assistant

Mental Health Associate or Worker

Mental Health Therapy Aide

Mental Health Community Service Worker

Mental Health Technician

Mental Health Technician/Social Worker

Mental Health Technologist

Mental Health Rehabilitation Worker

Psychiatric Aide

Psychiatric Technician

Community Health Worker

Community Mental Health Worker

Community Mental Health Assistant

Community Mental Health Associate

Community Mental Health Technologist

Community Services Associate

Health Resources Aide

Human Relations Worker

Human Services Worker

We see that, in general, paraprofessionals in psychiatry are involved as associates or aides in providing mental health and human resource services with social work, psychiatric, medical and nursing aspects to patients in hospitals, clinics and the community.

What is conspicuous by its absence is the job title "attendant"!

75

Therapeutic One-Liners I Find Useful

1. Be careful about what you say you want because you might get it!

2. Learn to accept the paradoxes and contradictions of life!

3. Don't make a federal case out of every little thing that happens in your life.

4. Don't expect what you only have a right to hope for.

5. It's better to see the glass half-full than half-empty!

6. Learn to look at people and situations with new eyes!

7. Have you tried seeing it from their point of view?

8. I don't have to justify this by explaining why I did it. I only have to examine what was going on at the moment and I'll know why.

9. Such as I am I can only do the best I can! Can you do more than the best you can do?

10. If I am not for myself who will be? But if I am only for myself, then what am I? And not later, but now!

11. A friend is someone who can "just" be with you—without having to "show you"—to "prove"—to "say the right thing."

12. To have friends, you have to make efforts to be a friend yourself.

13. It's helpful to ask yourself: "Am I doing this to prove or to improve?" "Am I doing this to impress or to express?"

14. When you feel angry and don't know why—you can sometimes find out by asking, "Am I doing this because I should—or because I want to?"

15. When caught up in unresolved conflict, ask yourself, "Do I have any other options? What are they?"

16. I can more quickly resolve certain conflicts by asking, "Which is the lesser of two evils?" rather than "Which solution is good and which is bad?"

17. If I suggest to myself that I will fail, I may set up a self-fulfilling prophecy and then proceed to enact the prophecy. Such prophecies are unfortunately the kind that lead to feeling "rejected," "victimized" or "ex-

ploited." I have to more often ask myself, "What was my role in setting up this self-defeating arrangement?"

18. When I stop forcing myself to try to remember the name which is on the tip of my tongue but I just can't remember it even though I'm trying desperately hard to remember it—I find that in the moment I let go—in the moment after I give up trying to remember—I then remember it!

19. It's better to learn now than never that practically everyone finds "life is hard." Life can become easier, but rarely easy. Ask the people you know if they find life to be easy and listen to what they say!

76

My Credo

Here is my credo. You can make your own credo by adding or substituting your own items as you discover what is important to you in working with people called patients.

I believe that in working with emotionally and mentally disabled persons I can best accomplish my mission (and I do acknowledge it as a mission) if I function *at appropriate times* by BEING:

1. Honest with what I state, but not having to state everything

2. Warm

3. Congruent

4. Interested—Listening—Observing

5. As accepting as possible in the situation

6. Aware of my "self"—and the "other" and what is "between" us

7. Forthright, bold and nervy, risking and confronting

8. Realistic

9. Intimate

10. Giving, Feeding, Caring, Helping, Sharing

11. Receiving, Asking

12. Frustrating when limit setting is indicated or required

13. Capable of sitting in abeyance (being patient), in a state of "masterful inactivity"

14. Stimulating, provocative, stirring the patient to new thoughts, feelings, insights and change

15. Hopeful

16. Flexible

17. Exhortative

18. Enthusiastic

19. Supportive without fostering continued dependency

20. Directive when safety or time considerations require it

21. Interpretive and reflecting back to the patient the meaning, implications or responses his behavior brings, has brought to him, or is liable to bring

22. Inspirational

23. Trusting

24. Permissive to a degree which doesn't impair the rights or safety of others as well as the patient

25. Loving

26. Human

And Always Present!

77 Selected Readings, Films and Videotapes

A PSYCHIATRIC GLOSSARY edited by Shervert H. Frazier, M.D. and others for the American Psychiatric Association Committee on Public Information in 1975. The most comprehensive up-to-date clarification of terms used in psychiatry. A must in your library.

TOWARD THERAPEUTIC CARE: A Guide for Those Who Work with the Mentally Ill. Publications Office, Group for the Advancement of Psychiatry, 419 Park Ave. South, NewYork, N.Y. 10016. A book for all those involved in 24-hour patient care.

THE COMMUNITY WORKER: A Response to Human Need. Publications Office, Group for the Advancement of Psychiatry, 419 Park Ave. South, New York, N.Y. 10016.

NEUROSIS AND HUMAN GROWTH by Karen Horney, M.D. Norton and Company, New York, 1950. Paperback available through Librarian, Karen Horney Clinic, 329 E. 62nd Street, New York, N.Y.10021. A comprehensive "down-to-earth" commonsense approach to understanding healthy and unhealthy personality and character development in our society. It offers insights for all who work with the mentally ill or in education as to what is involved in causing and giving up self-hate and excessive expectations of self and others, while developing healthy compassion and learning to use one's energies for "real-self" growth.

COMPASSION AND SELF-HATE by Theodore Rubin, M.D. David McKay, New York, 1975. A psychiatrist shares in a clearly stated fashion the many ways we can get rid of the monkeys-on-our-backs. He spotlights the often elusive components found in the web of self-hate, guilt and self-deprecation and offers practical suggestions to build self-esteem and a life with more joy. Highly recommended for everyone, especially patients and clients.

I'M O.K.—YOU'RE O.K. by Thomas A. Harris, M.D. Harper and Row, New York, 1969. This offers another way (based on the contributions of Eric Berne) to understand how children become programmed through parental injunctions and scripts to learn to play self-defeating or self-actualizing "games" in the struggle towards becoming a real person.

A MIND THAT FOUND ITSELF by Clifford W. Beers. Doubleday, New York, revised edition, 1971. This classic autobiography told in exquisitely poignant detail by a young man who recovered from insanity will help the newcomer to our field to understand the inner life of a person suffering with schizophrenia and depression. It is a chronicle of "seven hundred and ninety-eight days of depression" during which the author, a sensitive, intelligent person, "drew countless incorrect deductions. But, such as they were, they were deductions, and essentially the mental process was not other than that which takes place in a well-ordered mind." Clifford W. Beers knew how to turn his personal catastrophe into something positive and constructive. The story of how he founded and developed the mental hygiene movement is told in this book.

I NEVER PROMISED YOU A ROSE GARDEN by Hannah Green. New American Library Signet Paperbacks, 1964. This intimate, truthful account of what goes on inside a sensitive schizophrenic young woman in a mental hospital clearly reveals how the acceptance and human help of her therapist are rehabilitative.

PERSUASION AND HEALING: A Comparative Study of Psychotherapy by Jerome D. Frank, M.D. Schocken Books, New York, revised edition, 1974. This modern "classic" reviews and compares the common elements in all types of "healing" and "healers" from past to present. It is highly provocative as well as educative and gives us a continuing basis for hope in our work with patients and clients.

A GUIDE TO TREATMENT IN PSYCHIATRY by Phillip Polatin, M.D. J.B. Lippincott, Philadelphia, 1966. An older but excellent, comprehensive review of what's available in the way of examining, understanding and treating patients. Prepared by a meticulous scholar who devoted a lifetime to teaching at the New York State Psychiatric Institute.

SCHIZOPHRENIA: BIOLOGICAL AND PSYCHOLOGICAL PERSPECTIVES edited by Gene Usdin, M.D. Brunner/Mazel, Inc., New York, 1975. A readable, up-to-date overview of what we know about schizophrenia and of the different treatment approaches.

BODY LANGUAGE AND SOCIAL ORDER: Communication as Behavioral Control by Albert Scheflen, M.D. Prentice Hall, Englewood, N.J., 1973. The pictures as well as written content convey clearly how much we establish, maintain, and regulate in our relationships through our nonverbalized behaviors.

KINESICS AND CONTEXT: Essays on Body Motion Communication by Ray L. Birdwhistell. Ballantine Paperback, New York, 1970. This is a most comprehensive presentation of human communication, demonstrating how all our senses are used in communicating. Each group and subgroup of peoples develop patterns of communicating and codes to understand the cues, symbols, and patterns which amplify and qualify our words.

PSYCHIATRIC-MENTAL HEALTH NURSING EXAMINATION REVIEW BOOK by Francis B. Arje, Charlotte H. Martin and Irene L. Sell. Vol. II, 3rd Ed., Medical Examination Publishing Company, New York, 1972. A scholarly sequence of 1500 multiple choice questions designed to assist students in learning psychiatric history, facts of normal growth and development, psychopathology, and intervention techniques for providing basic care for persons with intellectual, emotional, or mental disorders. There are variations in test question format to familiarize the reader with various types of national board, state board and school examinations in current use. This book is too valuable to be restricted to nurses alone. All mental health workers will find it valuable.

WORKING WITH PEOPLE CALLED PATIENTS: A SIX-PART SERIES. Presents a series of six programs on patient care, intended for the continuing education of the psychiatric professional and paraprofessional. Uses simulated vignettes, actual patient interviews, and group discussions to explore a broad range of treatment and communication problems and to pursue solutions in a realistic, humane, and modern manner. Includes the following titles: *I'm With You; Tuning In; Activating a Psychogeriatric Group; A Dialogue With Paraprofessionals On Patient Care; A Dialogue With Patients On Patient Care; Patients and Paraprofessionals In a Dialogue on Patient Care*. All films in the series are available singly or in a total package. For information concerning rental or purchase of these and other topics, write to: The Department of Education and Training, South Beach Psychiatric Center, 777 Seaview Avenue, Staten Island, N. Y. 10305 (212-390-6131/6132)

I'M WITH YOU, Milton M. Berger, M.D. Discusses the need for the paraprofessional mental health worker to identify with and treat with understanding the needs and interests of patients and clients. Emphasizes the development of protherapeutic approaches and the avoidance of antitherapeutic approaches. Describes ways of encountering patients with an attitude of interest, warmth, and respect for their physical and emotional boundaries and delineates ways of communicating that respect. Uses simulated vignettes and actual patient interviews to demonstrate methods of treating troubled, socially inept, and uneducated people with compassion, in order to help them gain a realistic perspective on their lives. Remarks: This 30-minute program contains privileged data; it is intended for both professional and paraprofessional use. *I'm With You* is available on black & white 16mm film, and videotape in any format.

TUNING IN, Milton M. Berger, M.D. Focuses on the paraprofessional's ability to comprehend nonverbal behavior as communications of what a patient is thinking and what the nature of his imminent behavior will be. Emphasizes that nonverbal communication may often be more effective than the spoken word in revealing the patient's reactions to the health care worker and to the environment, as well as revealing his own internal perceptions. Uses simulated vignettes and patient interviews to show how nonverbal behaviors serve to establish, maintain, and regulate interpersonal relationships and function as an aid to monitoring the patient's therapeutic progress. Remarks: This 30-minute program contains privileged data; it is intended for both professional and paraprofessional use. *Tuning In* is available on black & white 16mm film, and videotape in any format.

ACTIVATING A PSYCHOGERIATRIC GROUP, Lynne Flexner Berger, A.T.R. Shows a therapist activating a group of previously state-hospitalized elderly people in a metropolitan residential center. Demonstrates the value of the therapist's enthusiastic and committed involvement with these "dumped" men and women as she moves them from passivity toward greater aliveness and enjoyment of themselves through music, games, exercise, free association, and fantasy. Presents an approach to stimulating people intellectually, physically, and emotionally in a group situation which could also be used with institutionalized children, participants in drug rehabilitation programs, and other people who are deficient in motivation and activity. Remarks: This 25-minute program contains privileged data; it is intended for both professional and paraprofessional audiences. It is available on videotape in any format.

A DIALOGUE WITH PARAPROFESSIONALS ON PATIENT CARE, Milton M. Berger, M.D. Presents a candid group discussion, under the leadership of a professional therapist, among the paraprofessional members of several psychiatric staffs. Covers a wide range of problems relating to patient care, including problems with the patients themselves, with fellow workers who have become too passive and complacent in their attitudes toward patients, and with administrators who seem to be too conservative, wishing only to maintain the *status quo*. Stresses the need for the individual paraprofessional to retain an active and committed approach to patient care and to remain creatively inspiring to patients despite the resistance among other staff members. Remarks: This 30-minute program does not contain privileged data; it is intended for both professional and paraprofessional audiences. It is available on videotape in any format.

A DIALOGUE WITH PATIENTS ON PATIENT CARE, Milton M. Berger, M.D. Shows a group of inpatients and outpatients in a discussion led by a therapist. Covers the patients' experiences in various psychiatric institutions over a period of many years. Reveals, through the patients' graphic descriptions of life in mental health facilities, situations in which their human needs and desires have been stifled by inhumane individuals and dehumanized environments. Presents via examples such as a female patient who follows instructions primarily for fear of punishment a clear indictment of what is wrong and a clear appreciation of what is right in treatment of the mental patient. Remarks: This 30-minute program contains privileged data; it is intended for professional and paraprofessional use. It is available on videotape in any format.

PATIENTS AND PARAPROFESSIONALS TALK ABOUT PATIENT CARE, Milton M. Berger, M.D. Presents a group discussion, guided by a therapist, among inpatients, outpatients, and paraprofessional staff members of past and present experiences in psychiatric institutions. Shows them speaking openly, from their several points of view, about both patient- and staff-caused problems, about difficulties stemming from inappropriate individual attitudes, and about the means by which patients and staff can be brought into greater cooperation. Covers such aspects as the relations between older patients and young staff members and the degree to which a sincere show of interest on the part of a single paraprofessional can benefit a patient's progress. Remarks: This 30-minute program contains privileged data; it is intended for both professional and paraprofessional audiences. It is available on videotape in any format.

PLANTING THINGS I WON'T SEE FLOWER, Clelia Goodyear, C.S.W. and Jeffrey Weber. Provides an intimate portrait of a family struggling with the demands forced upon them by terminal illness. It does not portray a family with comfortable answers or reflect persons who have come to terms with their "goodbyes." It offers a look at the dynamics of a family coping, however awkwardly, with their own needs and fears. Remarks: It stimulates discussion on dying and death amongst mental health workers and selected patients. It is available as a 26-minute 16mm color film and as a color ³/₄" video cassette through the United Methodist Film Service, 1725 McGavoc Street, Nashville, Tenn. 37203 (615-327-0911).

A FUZZY TALE, Claude Steiner, M.D. Presents the different kinds of positive and negative interpersonal "strokes" focused on in transactional analysis, as well as their importance in human relationships. Remarks: This 12-minute 16mm animated color film can stimulate discussion among all levels of mental health workers. It can be obtained through the United Methodist Film Service, 1725 McGavoc Street, Nashville, Tenn. 37203 (615-327-0911).

Index

153